RECORDED VERSIONS
GUITAR
AUTHENTIC TRANSCRIPTIONS
WITH NOTES AND TABLATURE

RED HOT CHILI PEP...

STADIUM ARCADIUM

MW00769895

Music transcriptions by Pete Billmann and David Stocker

ISBN-13: 978-1-4234-1580-0
ISBN-10: 1-4234-1580-9

HAL•LEONARD®
CORPORATION

7777 W. BLUEMOUND RD. P.O. BOX 13819 MILWAUKEE, WI 53213

In Australia Contact:
Hal Leonard Australia Pty. Ltd.
4 Lentara Court
Cheltenham, Victoria, 3192 Australia
Email: ausadmin@halleonard.com

Visit Hal Leonard Online at
www.halleonard.com

Dani California

Words and Music by Anthony Kiedis, Flea, John Frusciante and Chad Smith

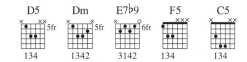

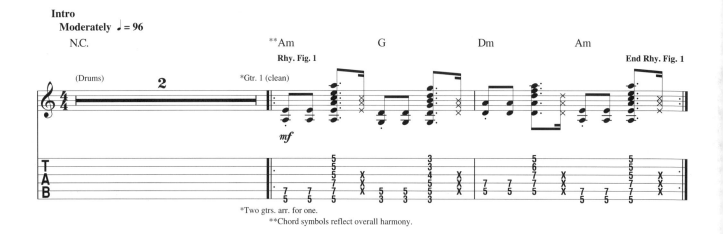

*Two gtrs. arr. for one.
**Chord symbols reflect overall harmony.

Verse

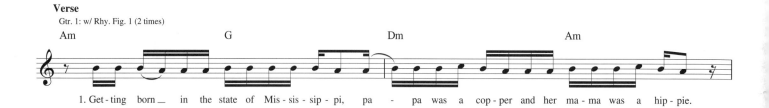

1. Get-ting born ___ in the state of Mis-sis-sip-pi, pa - pa was a cop-per and her ma-ma was a hip-pie.

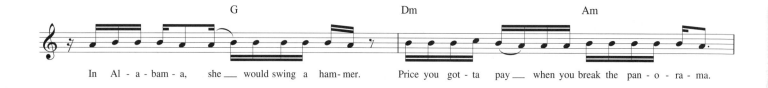

In Al - a - bam - a, she ___ would swing a ham-mer. Price you got-ta pay ___ when you break the pan - o - ra - ma.

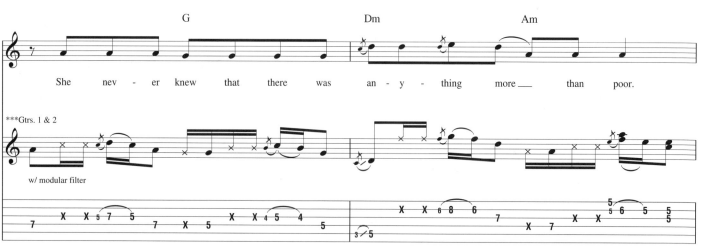

She nev - er knew that there was an - y - thing more ___ than poor.

***Gtr. 2 (clean), *mf.* Composite arrangement

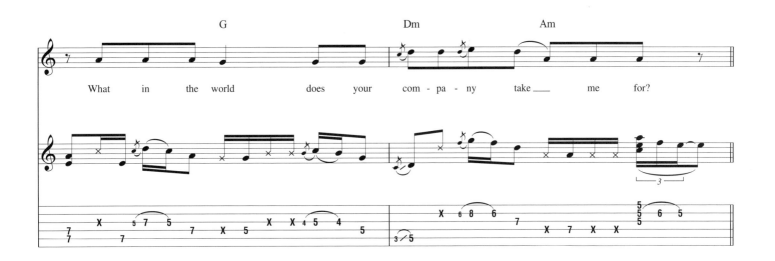

Verse

Gtr. 1: w/ Rhy. Fig. 1 (2 times)

Gtr. 2 tacet

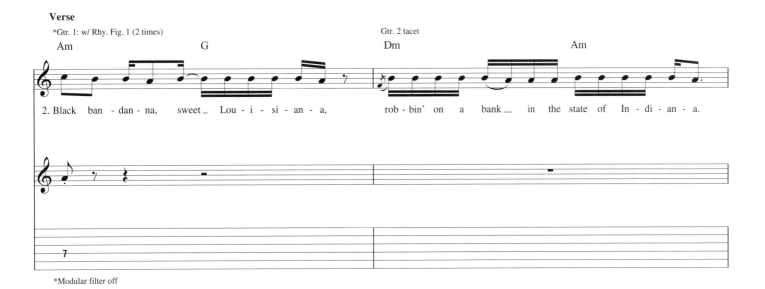

*Modular filter off

Riff A

**Gtrs. 1 & 2

w/ modular filter

End Riff A

**Composite arrangement

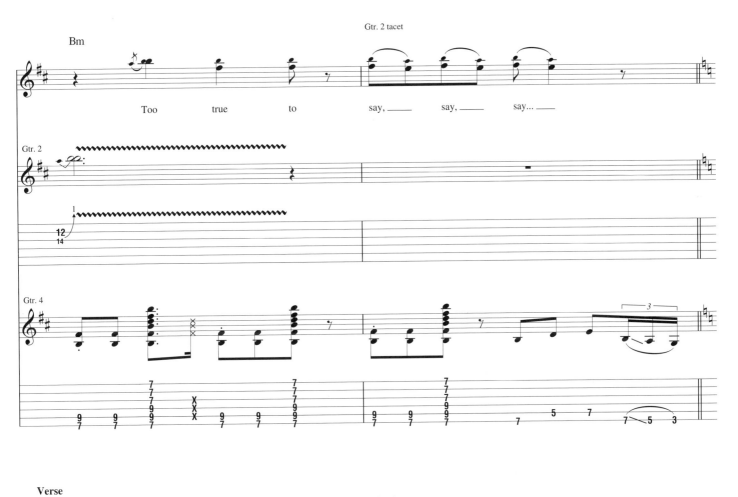

Too true to say, ____ say, ____ say... ____

Verse

Gtr. 1: w/ Rhy. Fig. 1 (2 times)

4. Push the fad - er, gift - ed an - i - ma - tor one ____ for the now ____ and e - lev - en for the lat - er.

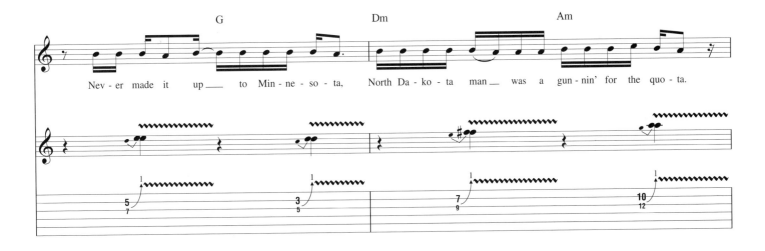

Nev - er made it up ____ to Min - ne - so - ta, North Da - ko - ta man ____ was a gun - nin' for the quo - ta.

Down in the Bad - lands, she was sav - in' the best ___ for last. It on - ly hurts when I laugh.

D.S. al Coda 2

Gone ___ too fast. _____ Cal - i - for -

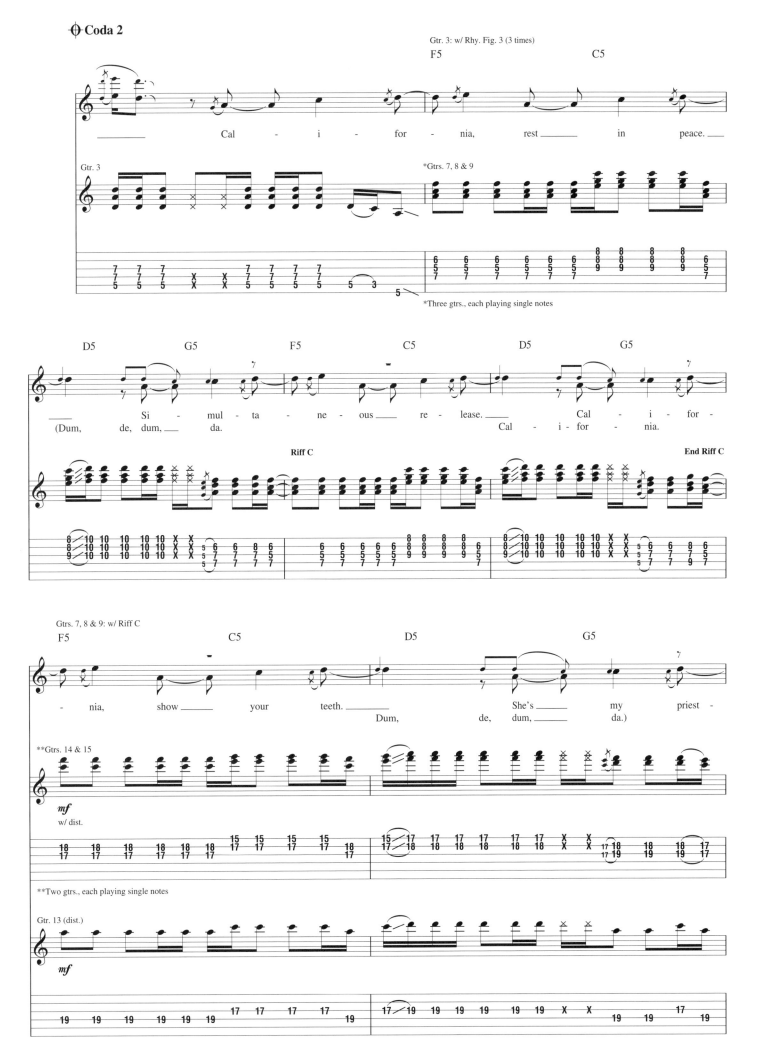

*w/ flanger on entire mix

Outro-Guitar Solo

Snow (Hey Oh)

Words and Music by Anthony Kiedis, Flea, John Frusciante and Chad Smith

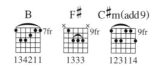

Intro

Moderately fast ♩ = 100

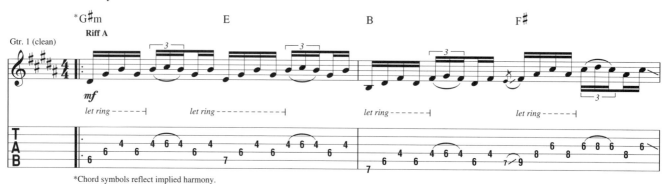

*Chord symbols reflect implied harmony.

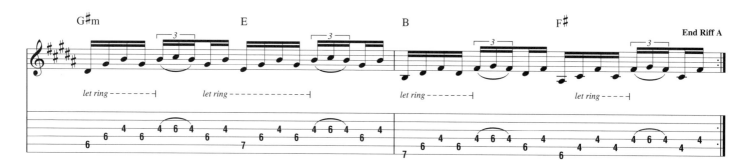

Verse

Gtr. 1: w/ Riff A (2 times)

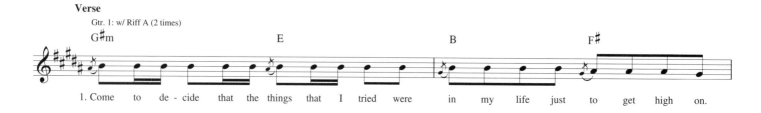

1. Come to de - cide that the things that I tried were in my life just to get high on.

When I sit a - lone come get a lit - tle known, but I need more than my - self this time.

Step from the road to the sea to the sky, and I do be - lieve that we re - ly on...

When I lay it on, come get to play it on all my life to sac - ri - fice.

Chorus

Gtr. 1: w/ Riff A (2 times)

Hey, oh, ___ lis - ten what I ___ say, ___ oh. ___ I got your

hey, oh, ___ now lis - ten what I ___ say, ___ oh, ___ oh. ___

Verse

Gtr. 1: w/ Riff A (2 times)

2. When will I know that I real - ly can't go to the well once more time to de - cide on?

Rhy. Fig. 1   End Rhy. Fig. 1

*Gtr. 2

mf

Melotron arr. for gtr.

Gtr. 2: w/ Rhy. Fig. 1 (3 times)

When it's kill-ing me, when will I real-ly see all that I need to look in - side? Come to be-lieve that I bet-ter not leave be -

fore I get my chance to ride. When it's kill-ing me, what do I real-ly need, all that I need to look in - side?

Chorus

Gtr. 1: w/ Riff A (2 times)
Gtr. 2: w/ Rhy. Fig. 1 (4 times)

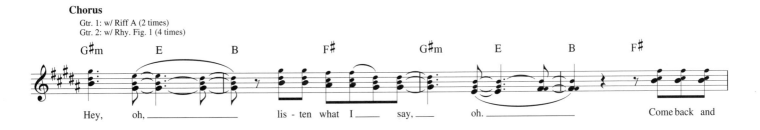

Hey, oh, ___ lis - ten what I ___ say, ___ oh. ___ Come back and

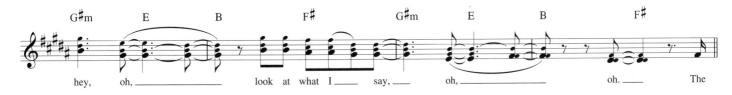

hey, oh, ___ look at what I ___ say, ___ oh, ___ oh. ___ The

Pre-Chorus

more I see the less __ I know, the more __ I like to let __ it go.

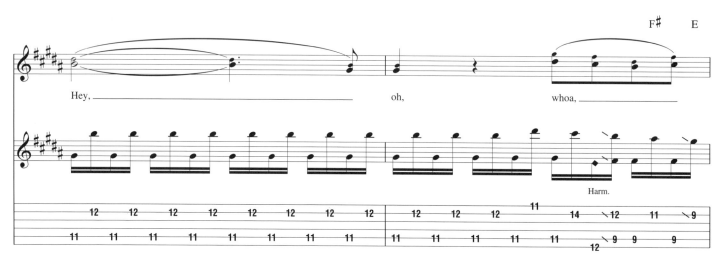

Hey, _____ oh, whoa, _____

whoa.

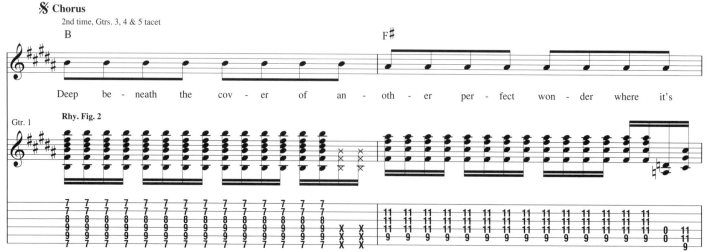

𝄋 Chorus
2nd time, Gtrs. 3, 4 & 5 tacet

Deep be-neath the cov-er of an-oth-er per-fect won-der where it's

14

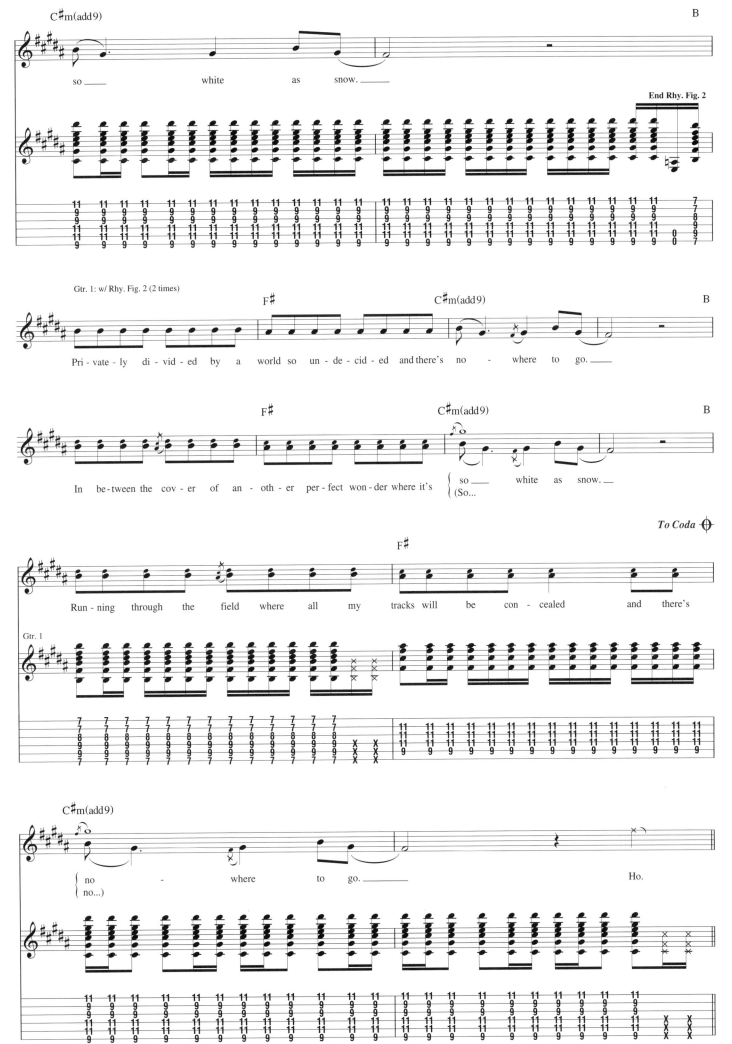

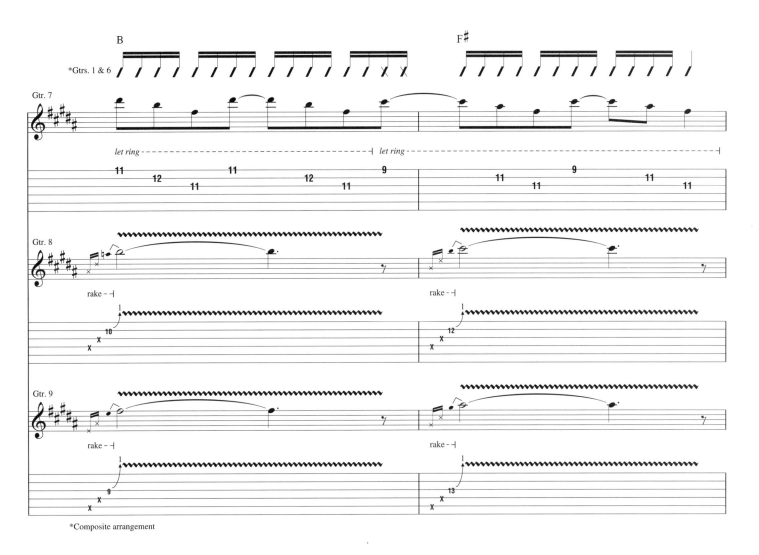

*Composite arrangement

Free time

Gtrs. 1, 6 & 7 tacet

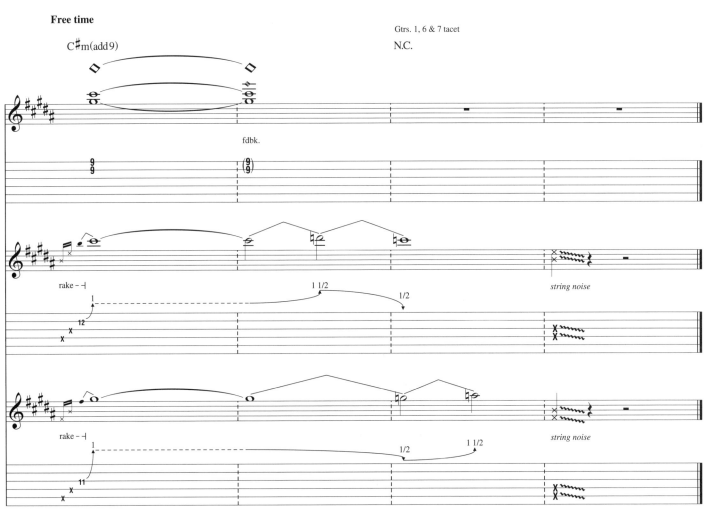

Charlie

Words and Music by Anthony Kiedis, Flea, John Frusciante and Chad Smith

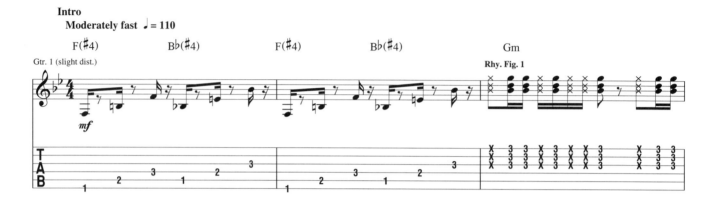

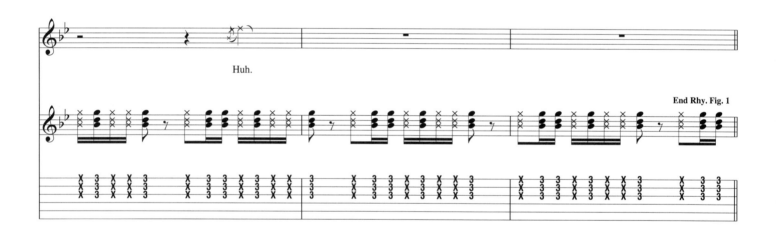

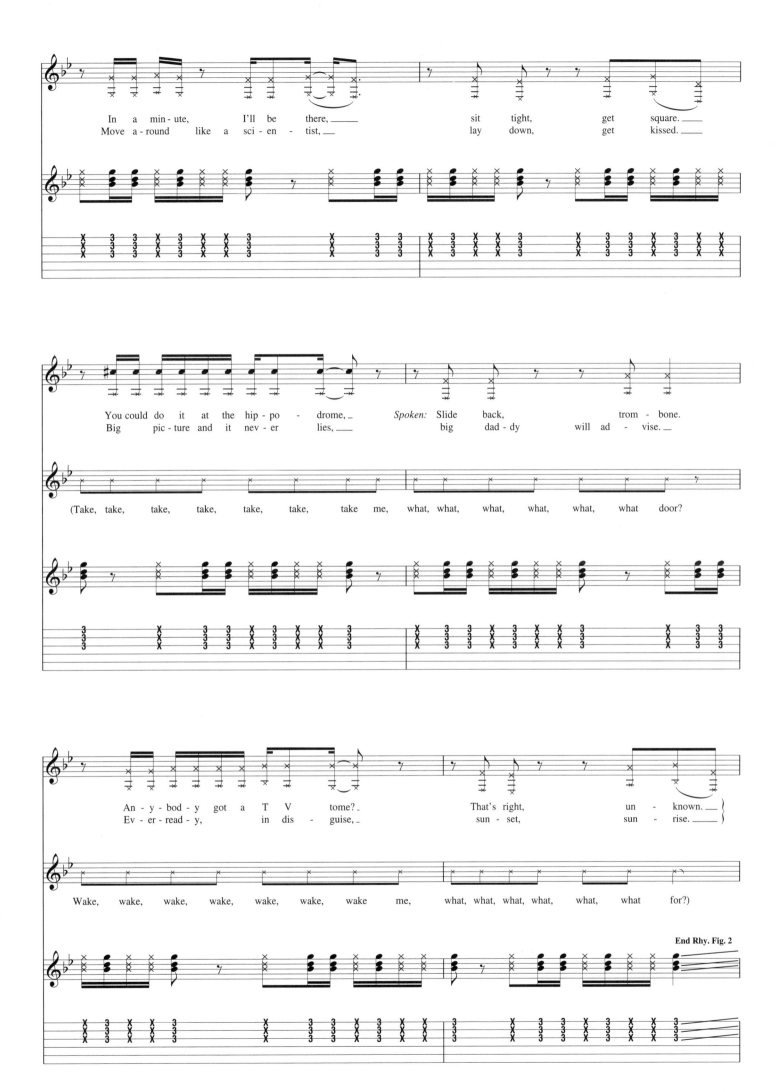

*2nd time, doubled at one octave higher.

**Synth. arr. for gtr.   ***Trem pick in septuplet sixteenth-note rhythm while sliding.

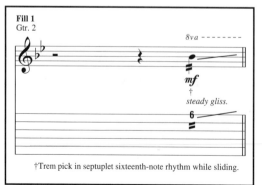

†Trem pick in septuplet sixteenth-note rhythm while sliding.

Interlude
Gtr. 1: w/ Rhy. Fig. 1

(Take, take, take, take, take, take, take me, what, what, what, what, what, what door?

Wake, wake, wake, wake, wake, wake, wake me, what, what, what, what, what, what for?)

⊕ Coda 1
Interlude
Gtr. 1: w/ Rhy. Fig. 3

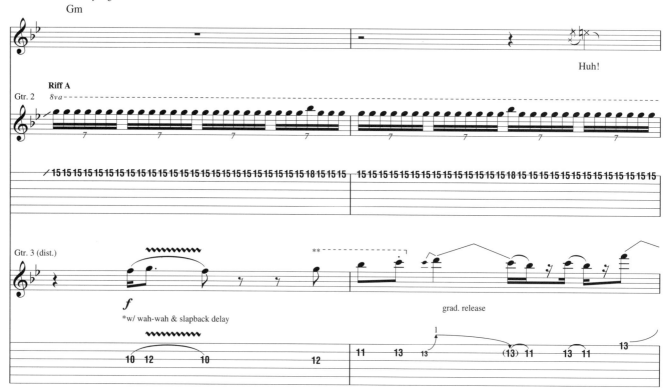

Huh!

Riff A

Gtr. 2 *8va*

Gtr. 3 (dist.)

f

*w/ wah-wah & slapback delay

grad. release

*Pan original signal hard left and delayed signal hard right.

**Played ahead of the beat.

End Riff A

8va

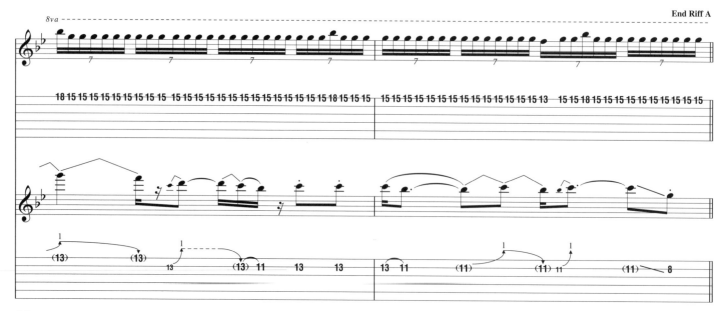

heart,   your   skin,   this   love   I'm   in.   We   don't   ar - rive   with -

out   a   sur - prise.   You're   right,   I'm   wrong,   be   free,   be - long.

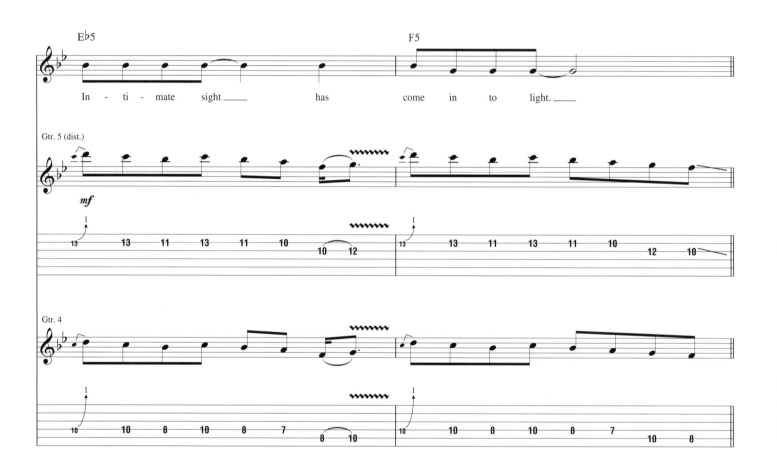

In - ti - mate   sight   has   come   in   to   light.

Pre-Chorus

Gtr. 1: w/ Rhy. Fig. 2
Gtr. 3 tacet

Gm

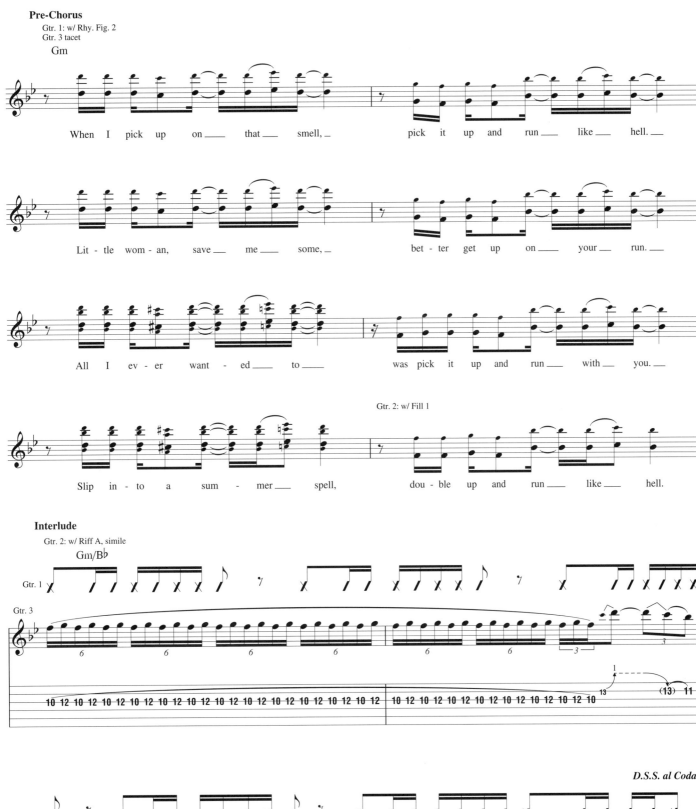

When I pick up on ___ that ___ smell, ___ pick it up and run ___ like ___ hell. ___

Lit - tle wom - an, save ___ me ___ some, ___ bet - ter get up on ___ your ___ run.

All I ev - er want - ed ___ to ___ was pick it up and run ___ with ___ you. ___

Gtr. 2: w/ Fill 1

Slip in - to a sum - mer ___ spell, dou - ble up and run ___ like ___ hell.

Interlude

Gtr. 2: w/ Riff A, simile

Gm/Bb

Gtr. 1

Gtr. 3

D.S.S. al Coda 2

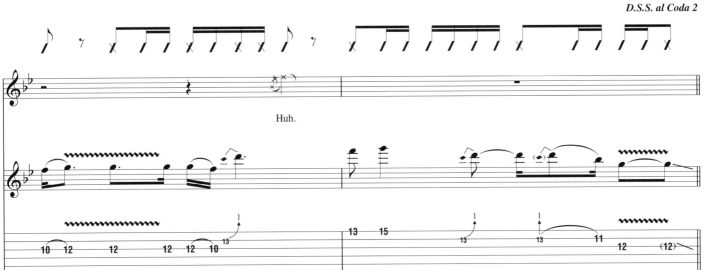

Huh.

Coda 2

Stadium Arcadium

Words and Music by Anthony Kiedis, Flea, John Frusciante and Chad Smith

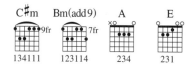

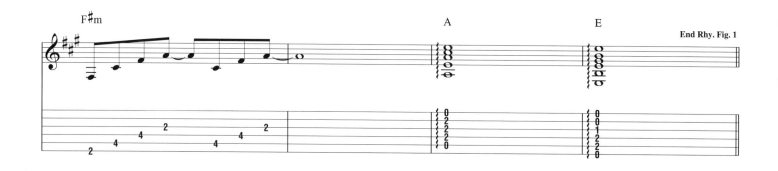

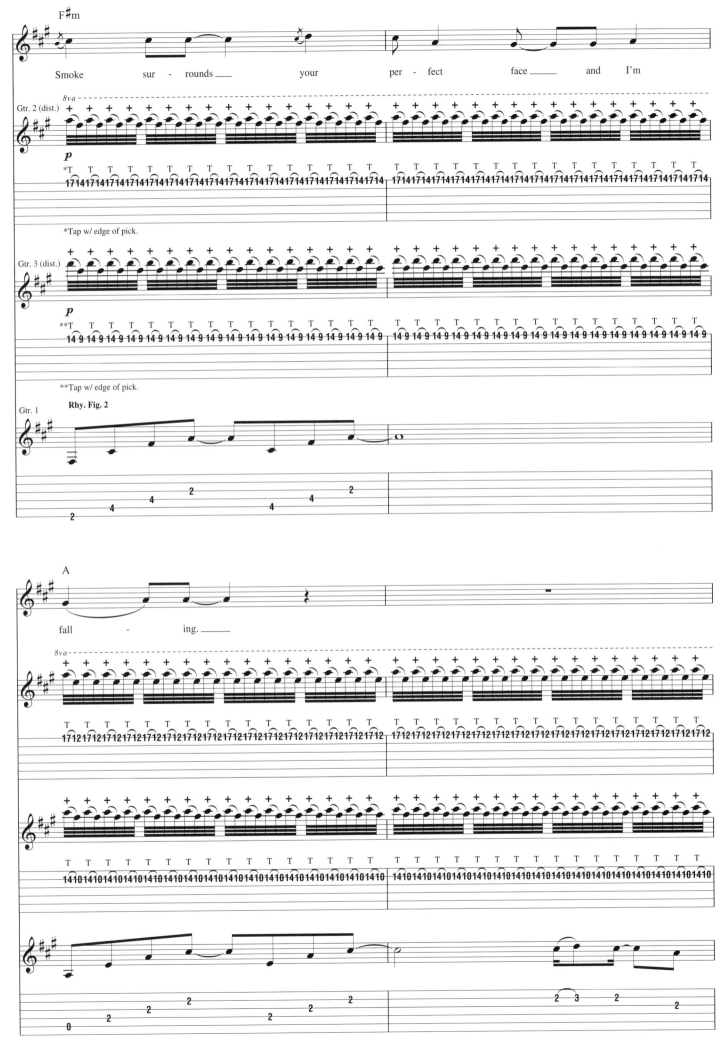

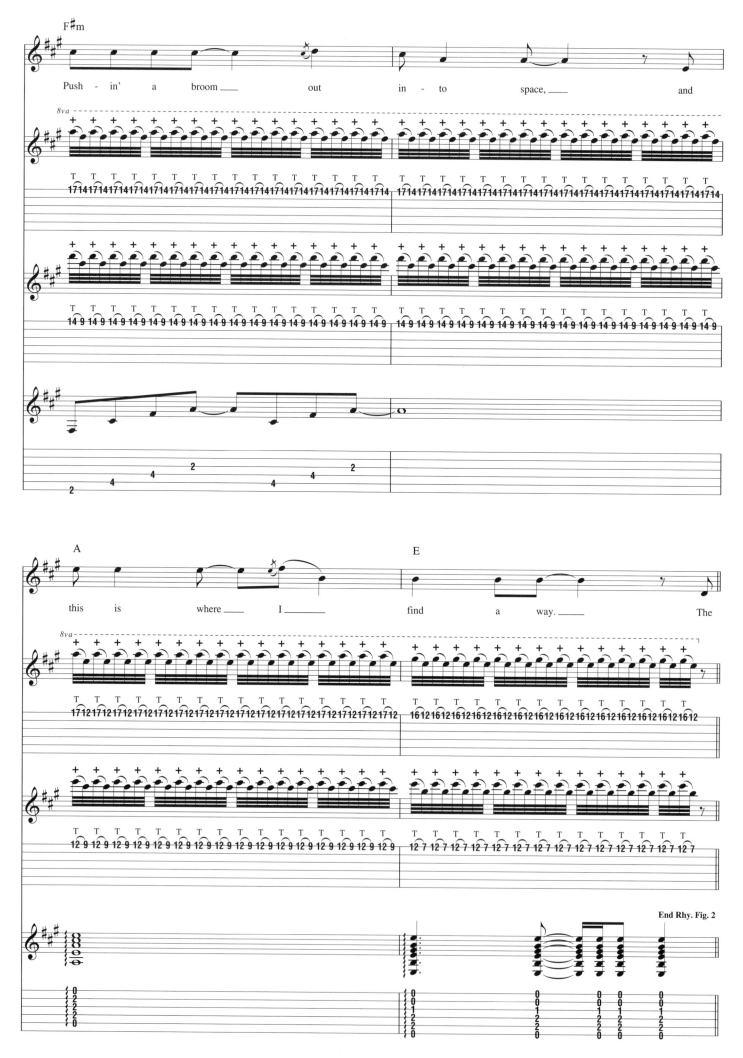

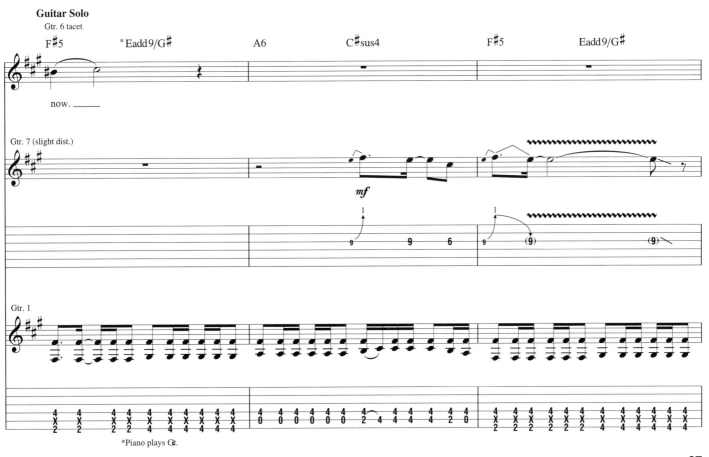

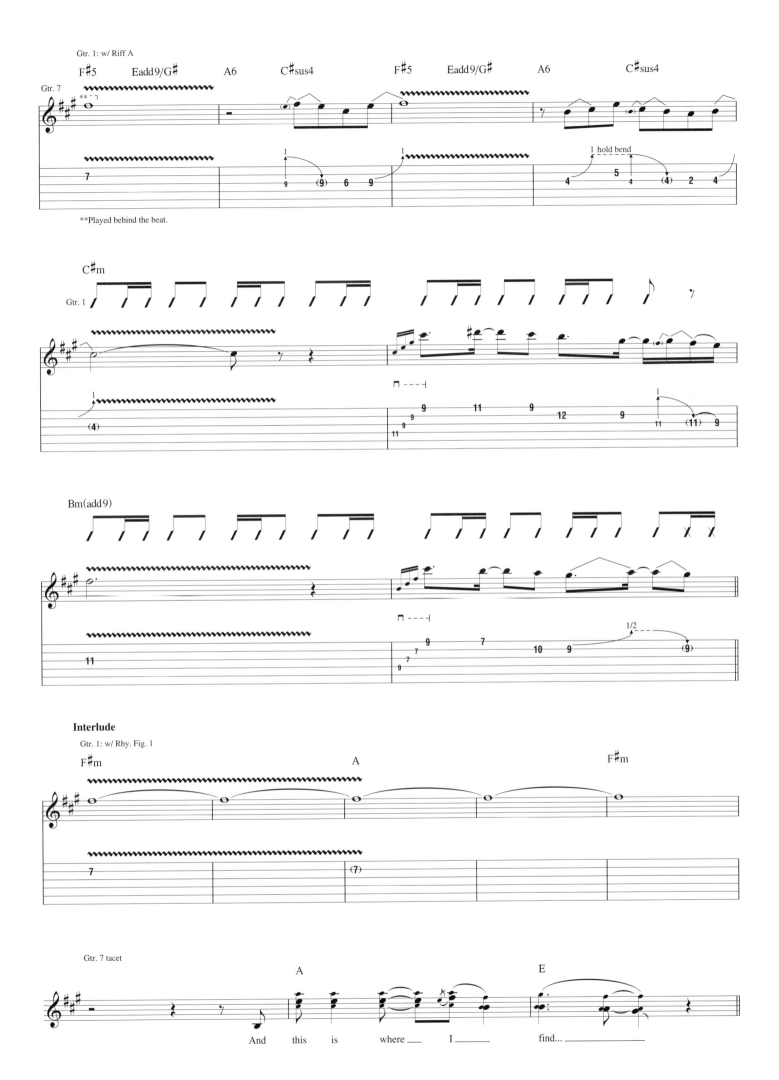

**Played behind the beat.

Interlude

Verse

Gtr. 1: w/ Rhy. Fig. 2

3. Rays of dust ___ that wrap a - round ___ your cit - i - zen. ___

D.S. al Coda

Kind e - nough ___ to dis - a - vow, ___ and this is where ___ I ___ stand. ___ The

Gtr. 6

Coda

Gtr. 1: w/ Rhy. Fig. 3 (last 2 meas.)
Gtr. 6: w/ Riff A (last 2 meas.)

push - in' my - self ___ and no, I don't mind ask - in'. The
you.) ___

Gtr. 8 (clean)

mp
let ring throughout

Outro-Chorus

Gtr. 1: w/ Rhy. Fig. 3 (1 1/2 times)
Gtr. 6: w/ Riff A (1 1/2 times)

sta - di - um ar - ca - di - um, ___ a mir - ror to ___ the moon. ___ And I'm ___
(Mir - ror to ___ the

Hump de Bump

Words and Music by Anthony Kiedis, Flea, John Frusciante and Chad Smith

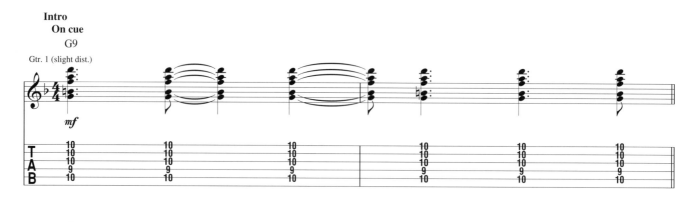

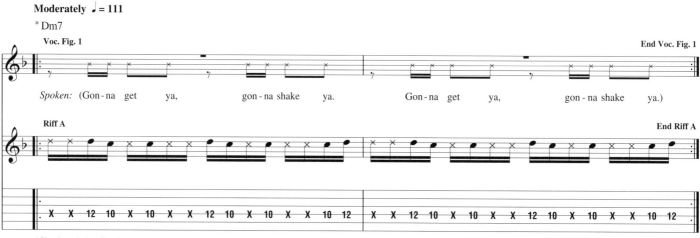

*Chord symbols reflect implied harmony.

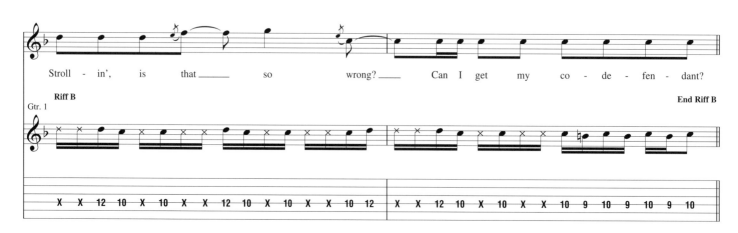

Pre-Chorus

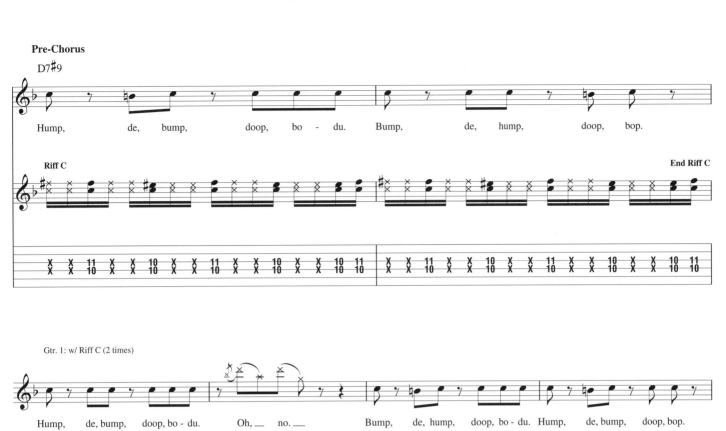

Hump, de, bump, doop, bo-du. Bump, de, hump, doop, bop.

Riff C ... **End Riff C**

Gtr. 1: w/ Riff C (2 times)

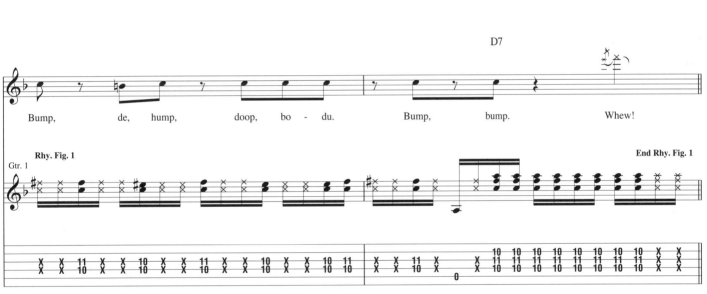

Hump, de, bump, doop, bo-du. Oh, __ no. __ Bump, de, hump, doop, bo-du. Hump, de, bump, doop, bop.

D7

Bump, de, hump, doop, bo-du. Bump, bump. Whew!

Rhy. Fig. 1 ... **End Rhy. Fig. 1**

Gtr. 1

Chorus

Dm   B♭7

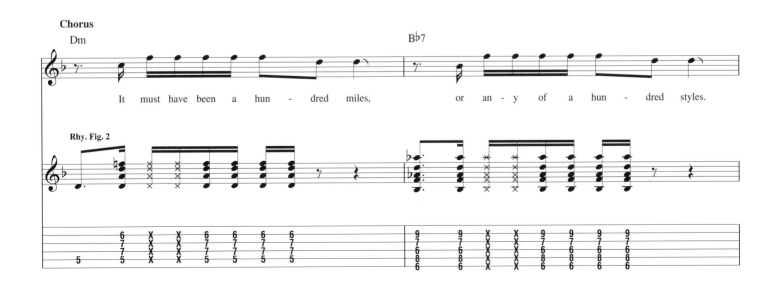

It must have been a hun-dred miles, or an-y of a hun-dred styles.

Rhy. Fig. 2

work - ing the belle _____ du monde. _____ Be -

lieve in the hav - oc we _____ wreak. Be - liev - in', is that _____ so wrong? _ Can I get my co - de - fen - dant?

𝄋 Pre-Chorus

Gtr. 1: w/ Riff C (3 times)

D7♯9

Hump, de, bump, doop, bo - du. Bump, de, hump, doop, bop.

*Trumpet arr. for gtr.

Gtr. 2: w/ Riff D (2 times)

Hump, de, bump, doop, bo - du.

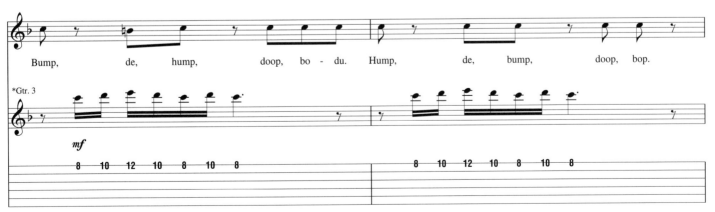

Bump, de, hump, doop, bo - du. Hump, de, bump, doop, bop.

*Trumpet arr. for gtr.

1st time, Gtr. 1: w/ Rhy. Fig. 1
2nd time, Gtr. 1: w/ Rhy. Fill 1

Bump, de, hump, doop, bo-du. Bump, bump, come on...

Chorus

Gtr. 1: w/ Rhy. Fig. 2
Gtrs. 2 & 3 tacet

It must have been a hun-dred miles, an-y of a hun-dred styles.
A, lis-ten to me what I said a, try to get it through your head.

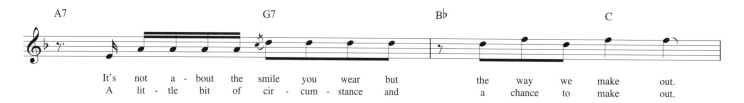

It's not a-bout the smile you wear but the way we make out.
A lit-tle bit of cir-cum-stance and a chance to make out.

1st time, Gtr. 1: w/ Rhy. Fig. 3
2nd time, Gtr. 1: w/ Rhy. Fig. 2

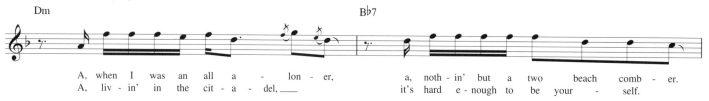

A, when I was an all a-lon-er, a, noth-in' but a two beach comb-er.
A, liv-in' in the cit-a-del, ___ it's hard e-nough to be your-self.

To Coda

Percussion Solo

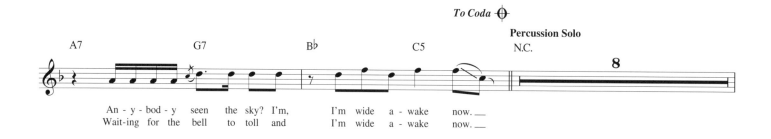

An-y-bod-y seen the sky? I'm, I'm wide a-wake now. ___
Wait-ing for the bell to toll and I'm wide a-wake now. ___

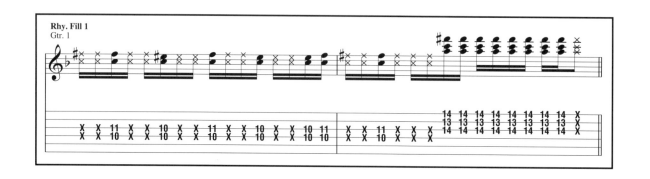

46

She's Only 18

Words and Music by Anthony Kiedis, Flea, John Frusciante and Chad Smith

- est minds and light will ____ shed. ____

Riff C2
Gtr. 4 (dist.)

mf

End Riff C2

Riff C
Gtr. 2

End Riff C

Gtr. 3
divisi
Riff C1

End Riff C1

Interlude
Gtr. 1: w/ Riff A (2 times)
Gtrs. 2, 3 & 4 tacet

Gm7   C5   Gm7   F5

Verse
Gtr. 1: w/ Riff A (2 times)

Gm7   C5   Gm7   F5

2. I heard some P - funk out on the road a - gain. ____ To get your head shrunk is what I rec - om - mend. ____

Gm7   C5   Gm7   F5

It's in your blood - line, a per - fect Frank - en - stein. ____ Out on that lone pine I'm gon - na make you mine.

Gtr. 1

Gtr. 1: w/ Riff B

Gm7   C5   Gm7   F5

It's un - der - stood, you wrap your voo-doo right a - round my neck. You've got some glit - ter on your kit - ty at the dis - co - theque.

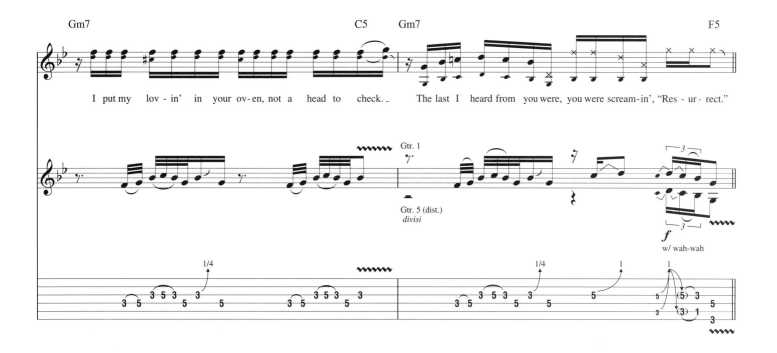

I put my lov - in' in your ov - en, not a head to check. _ The last I heard from you were, you were scream-in', "Res - ur - rect."

Gtr. 1

Gtr. 5 (dist.)
divisi

f
w/ wah-wah

Chorus
Gtr. 1 tacet
Gtrs. 2 & 3: w/ Rhy. Fig. 1

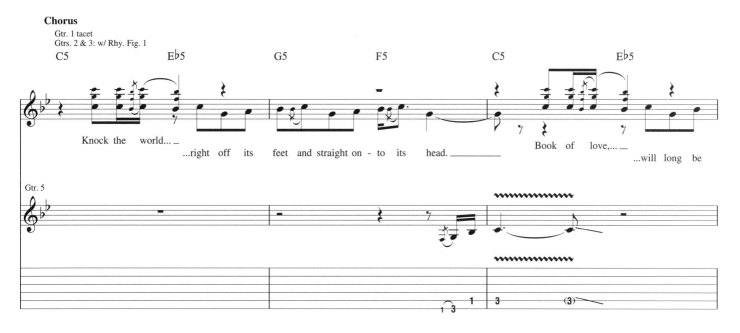

Knock the world... _ ...right off its feet and straight on - to its head. _____ Book of love,... _ ...will long be

Gtr. 5

laugh-ing af - ter you _ are dead. _____ Fas - ci - nat - ed... ...by the look _ of you and what was said. _____

Make a play,.... ...for all the bright - est minds and light will shed. _____ Who. _

Slow Cheetah

Words and Music by Anthony Kiedis, Flea, John Frusciante and Chad Smith

Gtrs. 1 - 3: Capo VI

Intro
Moderately slow ♩ = 88

Whispered: One, two, three, four.

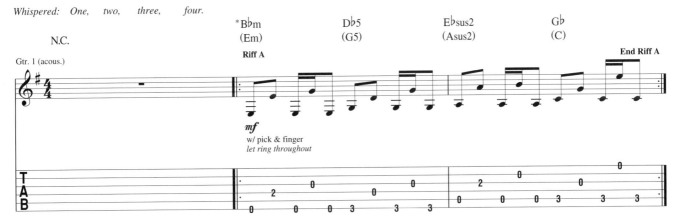

*Symbols in parentheses represent chord names respective to capoed guitar.
Symbols above represent actual sounding chords. Capoed fret is "0" in tab.
Chord symbols reflect implied harmony.

Verse
Gtr. 1: w/ Riff A (2 times)

1. Wak-in' up dead in-side — of my head would nev - er, nev-er do. There is no med, no med-i-cine to take. ____

I've had a chance to be — in - sane, a-sy - lum from the fall - ing rain.

I've had a chance to break.

End Riff B

Interlude

2nd time, Gtr. 1: w/ Riff A
2nd time, Gtr. 2 tacet

Gtr. 1: w/ Riff A

Riff C

Gtr. 1

End Riff C

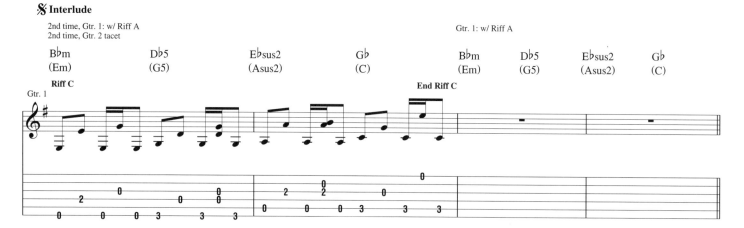

Verse

Gtr. 1: w/ Riff A

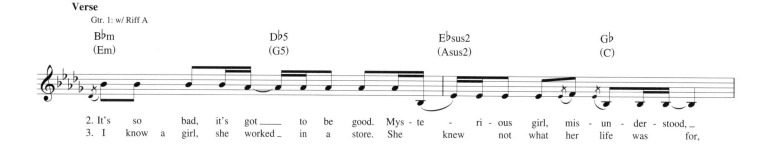

2. It's so bad, it's got ___ to be good. Mys - te - ri - ous girl, mis - un - der - stood, ___
3. I know a girl, she worked ___ in a store. She knew not what her life was for,

Gtr. 1: w/ Riff C

Gtr. 1: w/ Riff B (1st 3 meas.)

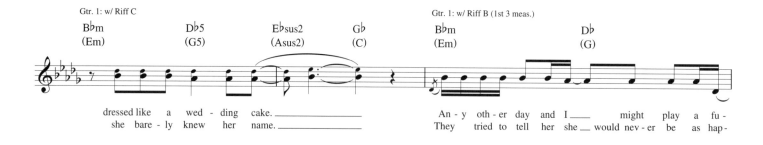

dressed like a wed - ding cake. ___
she bare - ly knew her name. ___

An - y oth - er day and I ___ might play a fu -
They tried to tell her she ___ would nev - er be as hap -

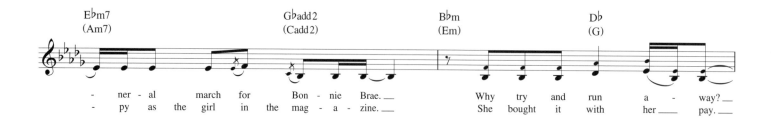

- ner - al march for Bon - nie Brae. ___
- py as the girl in the mag - a - zine. ___

Why try and run a - way?
She bought it with her ___ pay. ___

*Composite arrangement

Verse

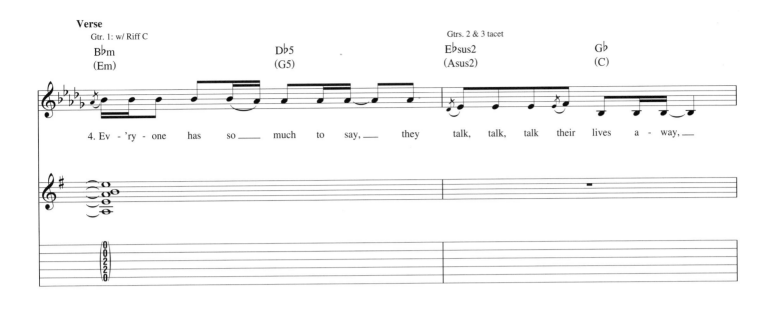

4. Ev-'ry-one has so ____ much to say, ____ they talk, talk, talk their lives a - way, ____

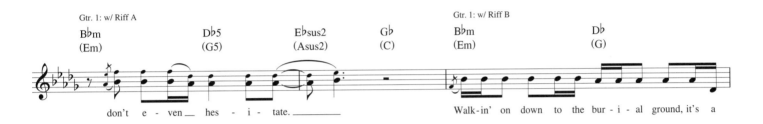

don't e - ven ____ hes - i - tate. ____ Walk-in' on down to the bur - i - al ground, it's a

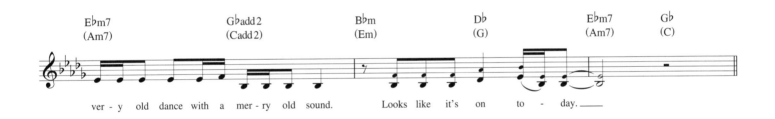

ver - y old dance with a mer - ry old sound. Looks like it's on to - day. ____

Interlude

Gtr. 1: w/ Rhy. Fig. 1

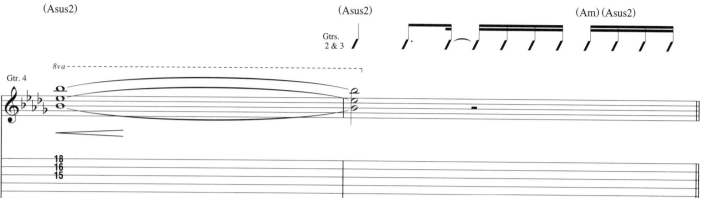

Chorus

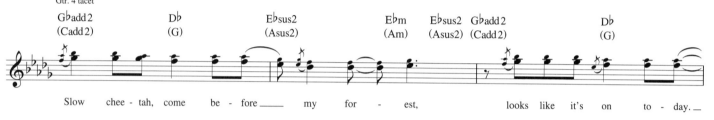

Slow chee-tah, come be-fore ___ my for-est, looks like it's on to-day. ___

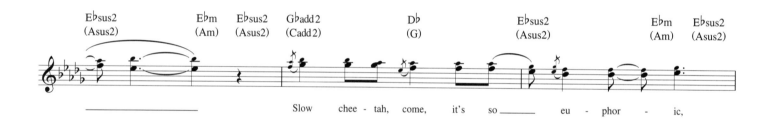

___ Slow chee-tah, come, it's so ___ eu-phor-ic,

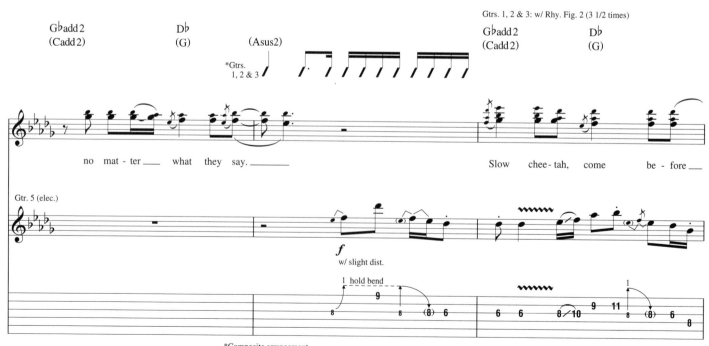

no mat-ter ___ what they say. ___ Slow chee-tah, come be-fore ___

*Composite arrangement

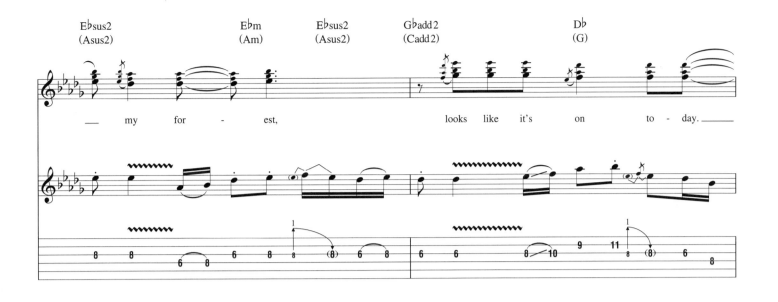

_my for - est, looks like it's on to - day. ____

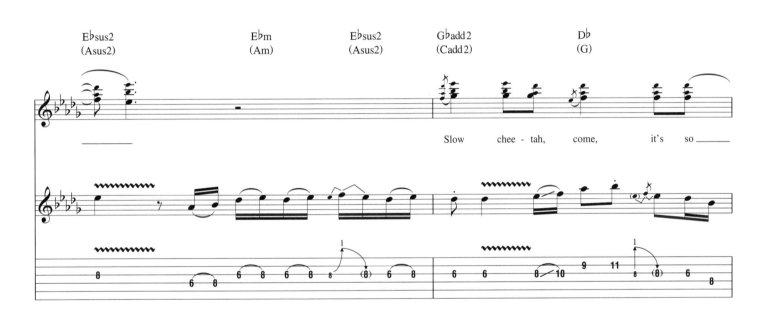

____ Slow chee - tah, come, it's so _____

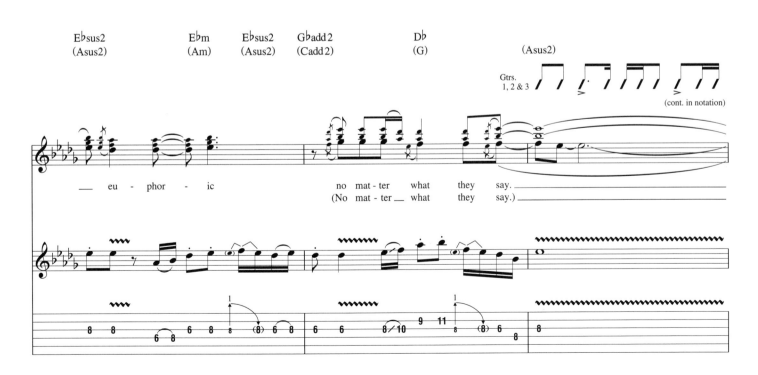

____ eu - phor - ic no mat - ter what they say. _____
(No mat - ter ____ what they say.) _____

Torture Me

Words and Music by Anthony Kiedis, Flea, John Frusciante and Chad Smith

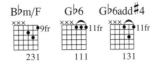

*Chord symbols reflect implied harmony.

**Bass arr. for gtr.

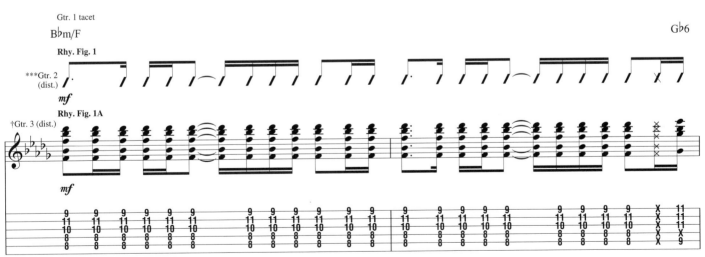

***Two gtrs. arr. for one.

†Two gtrs. arr. for one.

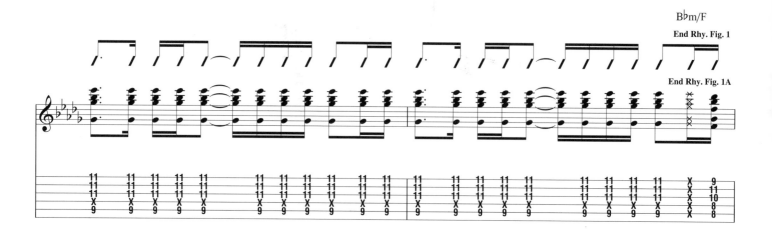

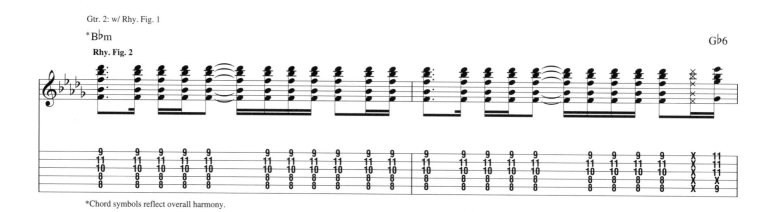

*Chord symbols reflect overall harmony.

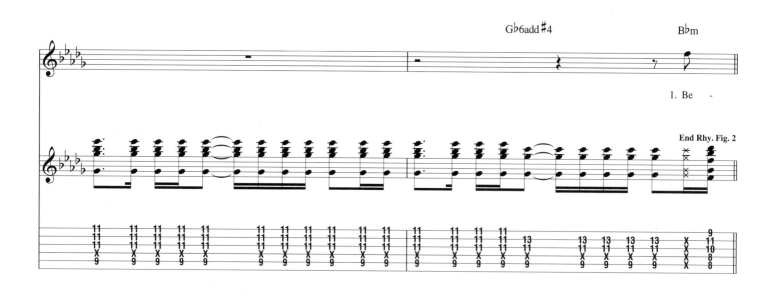

cause I'm hap-py to be sad___ I want it all, I want it bad.___ Oh.___

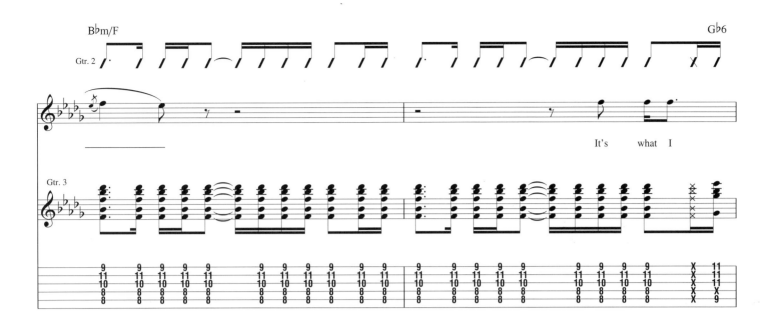

It's what I

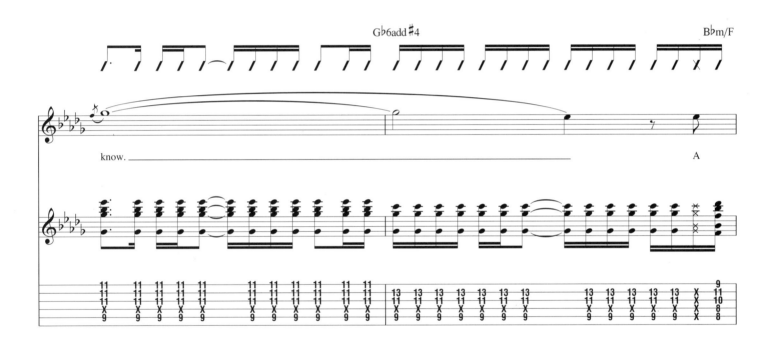

know. _____

A

Gtrs. 2 & 3: w/ Rhy. Figs. 1 & 1A (1 1/2 times)

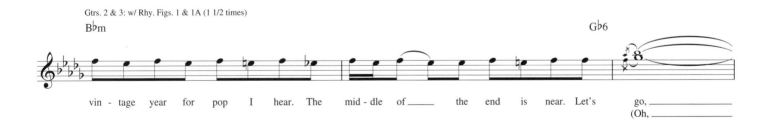

vin - tage year for pop I hear. The mid - dle of ___ the end is near. Let's go, _____
(Oh, _____

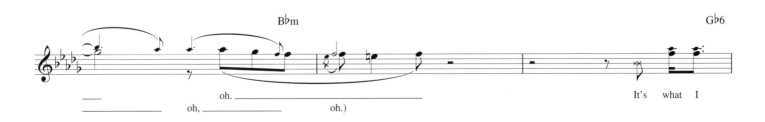

___ oh. _____

It's what I

_____ oh, _____ oh.)

Interlude

Gtr. 2: w/ Rhy. Fig. 1 (2 times)
Gtr 3: w/ Rhy. Fig. 2 (2 times)

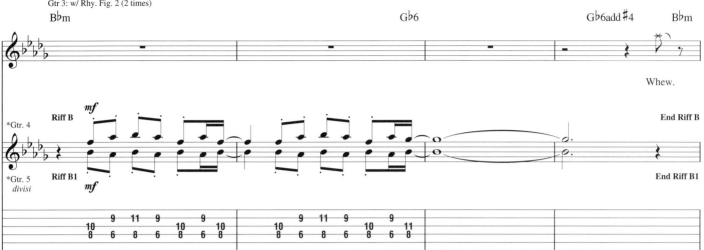

Whew.

*Gtr. 4 — Riff B — End Riff B
*Gtr. 5 — Riff B1 — End Riff B1
divisi

*Trumpets arr. for gtr.

Gtrs. 4 & 5: w/ Riffs B & B1

Verse

Gtrs. 2 & 3: w/ Rhy. Figs. 1 & 1A (1 1/2 times)

2. All the leaves are turn-ing brown, the wind is push-in' me a-round. __ Let's go. __
(Oh, __ oh, __

Gtrs. 2 & 3: w/ Rhy. Fills 1 & 1A

__ oh.)

It's what I know. __

Chorus

Gtr. 3: w/ Riff A

Tor-ture me __ and tor-ture me. __ It's forc-in' me, __ so tor-ture me, __ please.

Riff C — End Riff C
Gtr. 2

turn it up __ and dumb it down, __ the vi - sion of your ul - tra - sound is so... _____ And

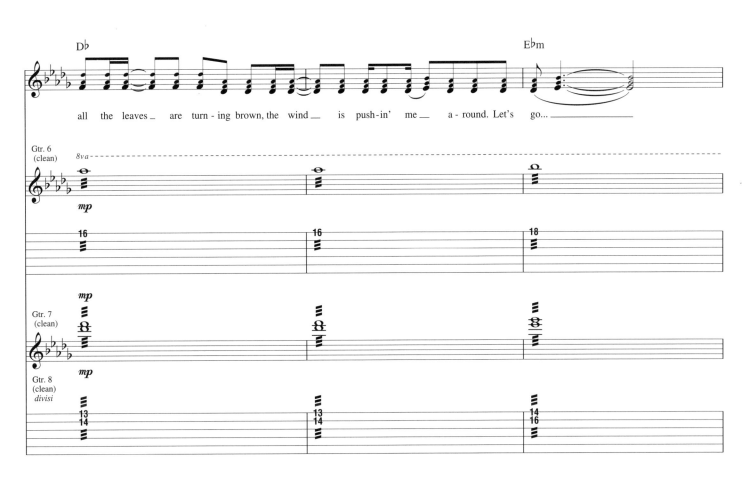

all the leaves __ are turn - ing brown, the wind __ is push - in' me __ a - round. Let's go... _____

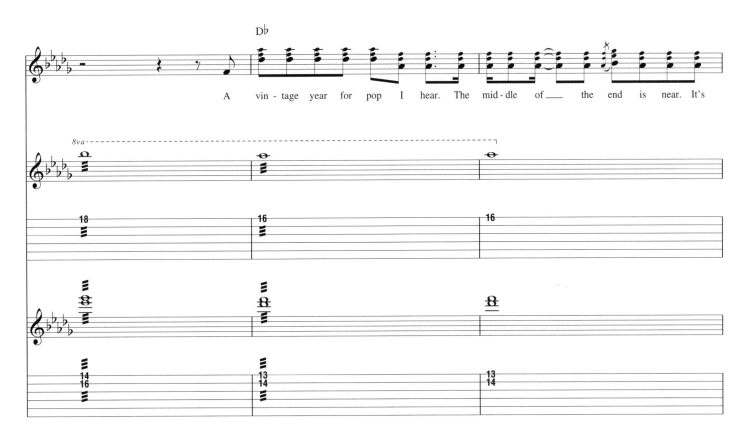

A vin - tage year for pop I hear. The mid - dle of __ the end is near. It's

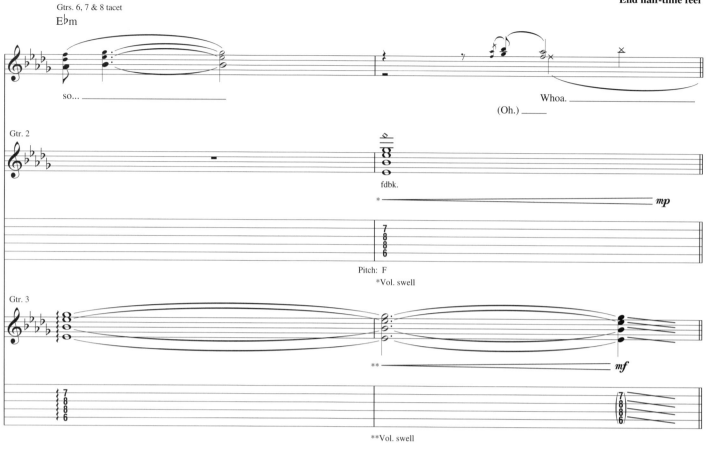

Guitar Solo

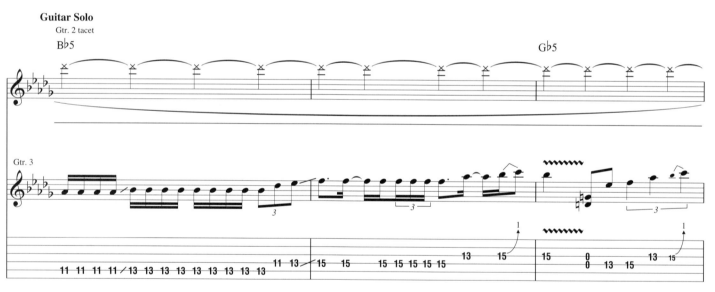

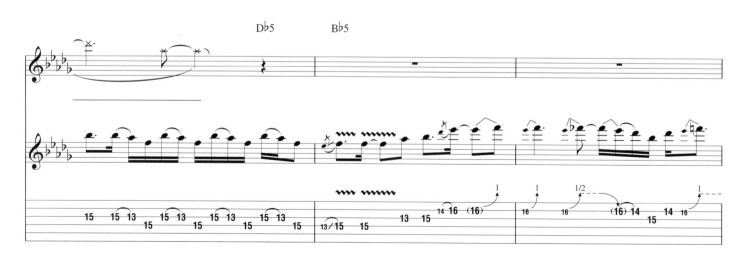

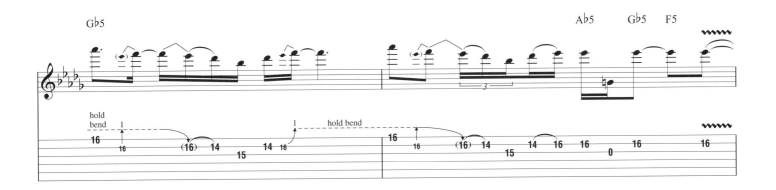

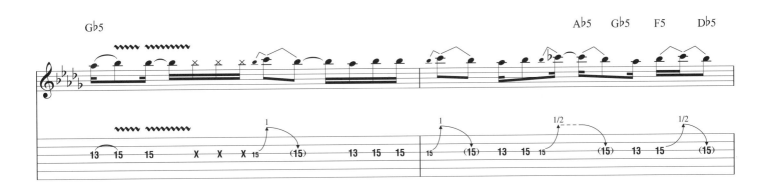

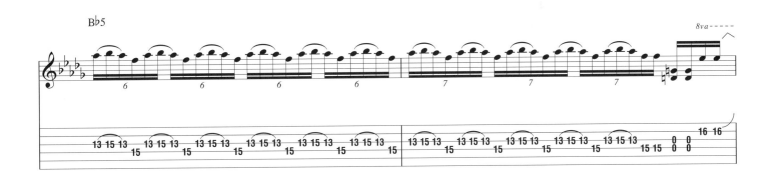

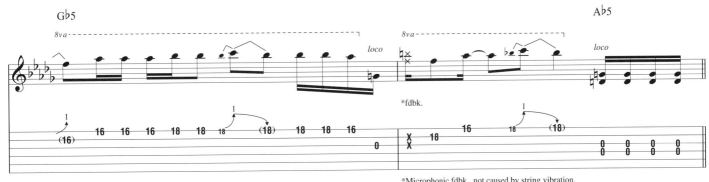

*Microphonic fdbk., not caused by string vibration.

Chorus

Free time

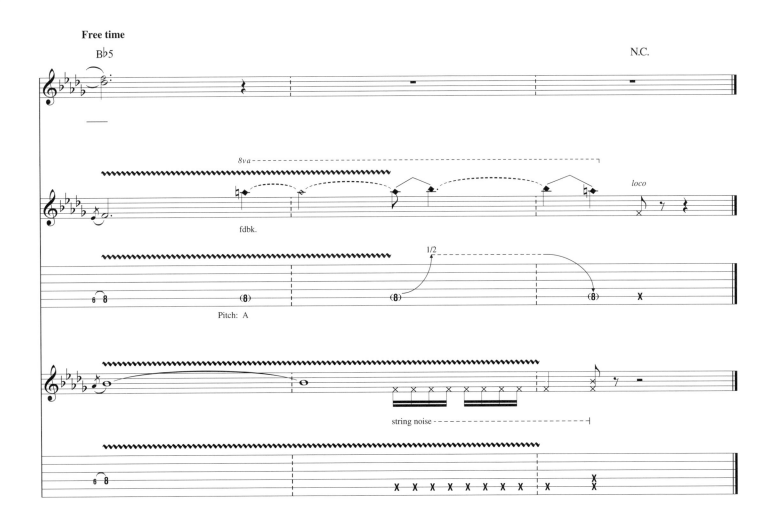

Strip My Mind

Words and Music by Anthony Kiedis, Flea, John Frusciante and Chad Smith

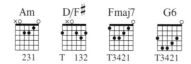

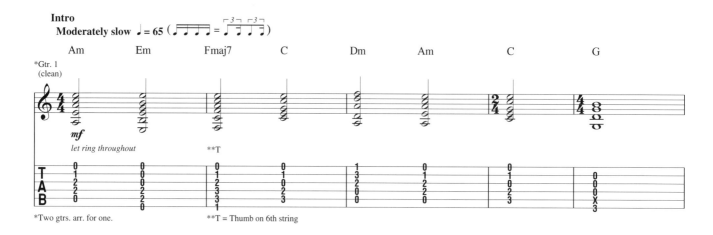

*Two gtrs. arr. for one.   **T = Thumb on 6th string

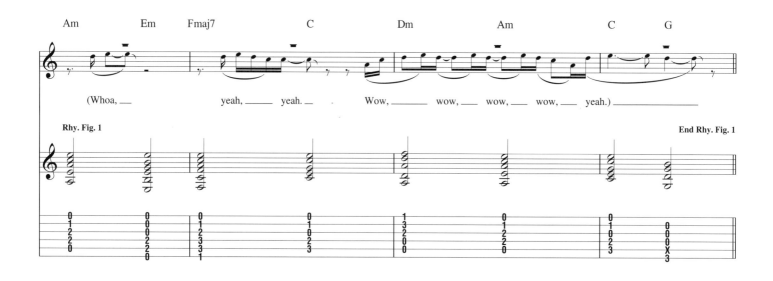

(Whoa, ___ yeah, ___ yeah. ___ Wow, ___ wow, ___ wow, ___ wow, ___ yeah.)

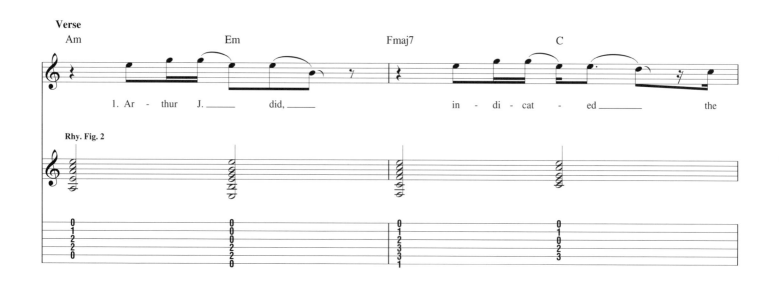

1. Ar - thur J. ___ did, ___ in - di - cat - ed ___ the

Spoken: Aw, say goodbye to your boots, man.

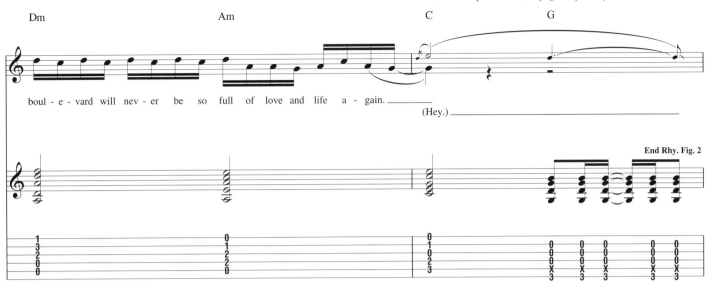

boul - e - vard will nev - er be so full of love and life a - gain. _____
(Hey.) _____

End Rhy. Fig. 2

Gtr. 1: w/ Rhy. Fig. 1

Hot as Ha - des, _____ ear - ly eight - ies. _____

Spoken: You gotta lose to win.

Sing an - oth - er song, ___ make me feel like I'm in love a - gain. _____
(Hey.) _____

Pre-Chorus

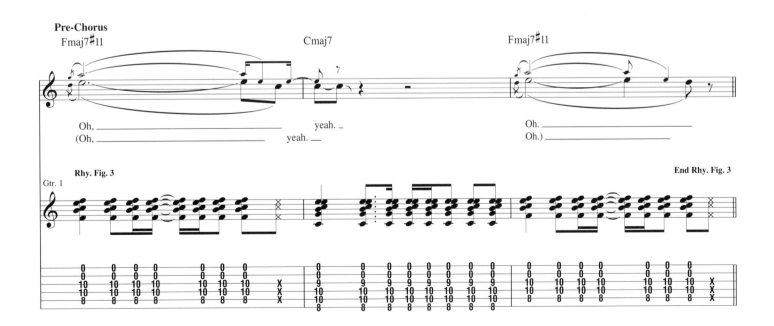

Oh, _____ yeah. _
(Oh, _____ yeah. _

Oh.
Oh.)

Rhy. Fig. 3

Gtr. 1

End Rhy. Fig. 3

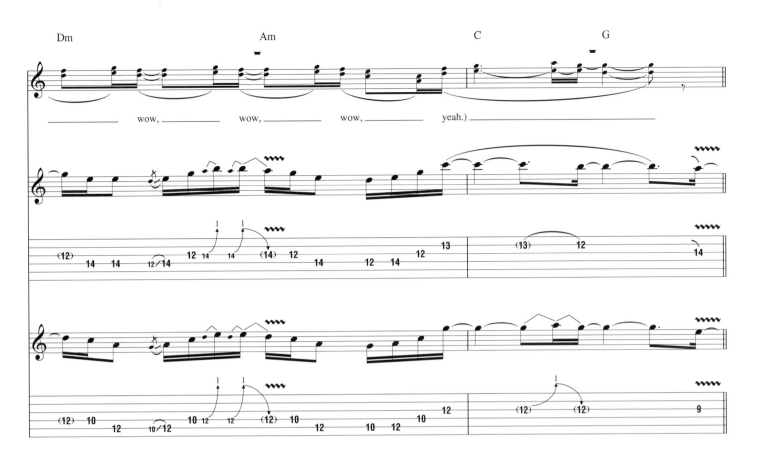

Verse
Gtr. 1: w/ Rhy. Fig. 2

Gtrs. 2 & 3 tacet

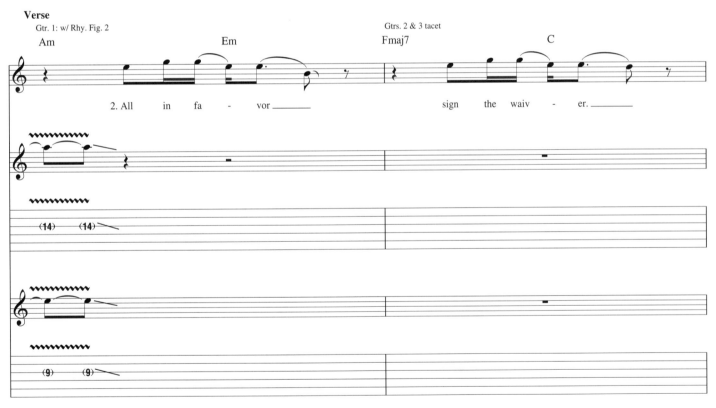

2. All in fa - vor _____ sign the waiv - er. _____

Spoken: Aw, it will make me cry.

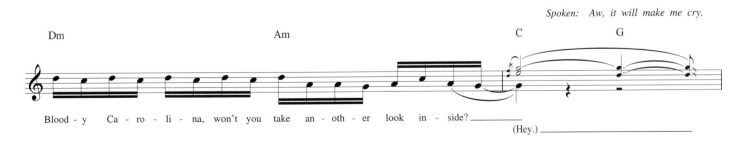

Blood - y Ca - ro - li - na, won't you take an - oth - er look in - side? _____

(Hey.)

*Each gtr. plays single notes.

*Chord symbols reflect harmony implied by bass (next 8 meas.).

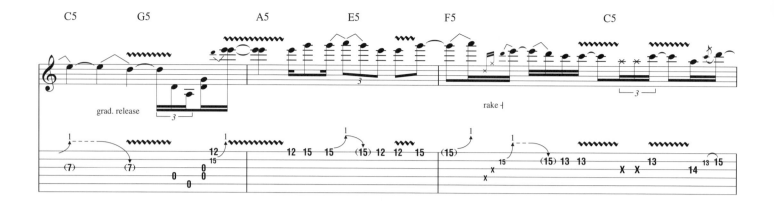

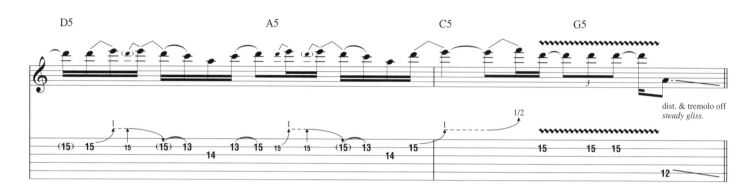

Verse

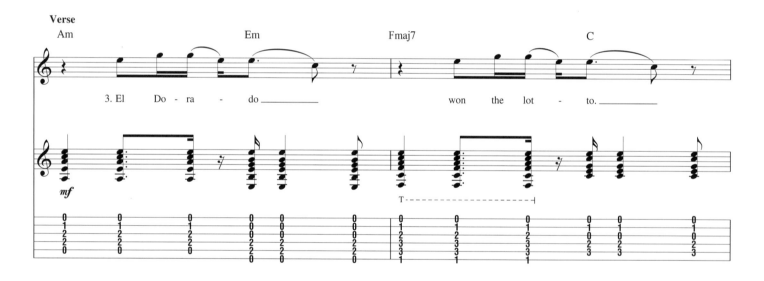

3. El Do - ra - do _____ won the lot - to. _____

All the cash and not a clue, but now you know what I've been through. _____

(Hey.) _____

Especially in Michigan

Words and Music by Anthony Kiedis, Flea, John Frusciante and Chad Smith

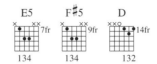

*Chord symbols reflect overall harmony.

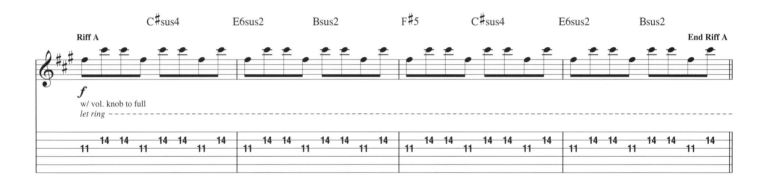

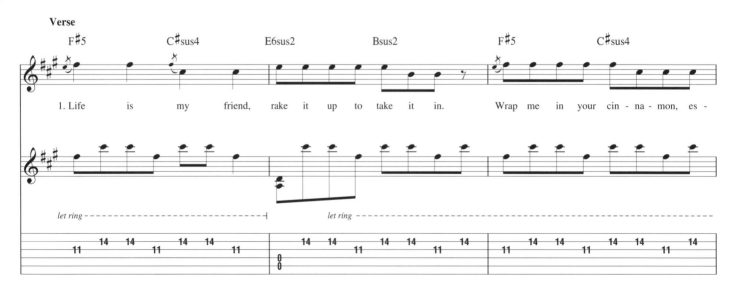

Chorus

Cry me a fu - ture where the rev - e - la - tions run a - mok, ___

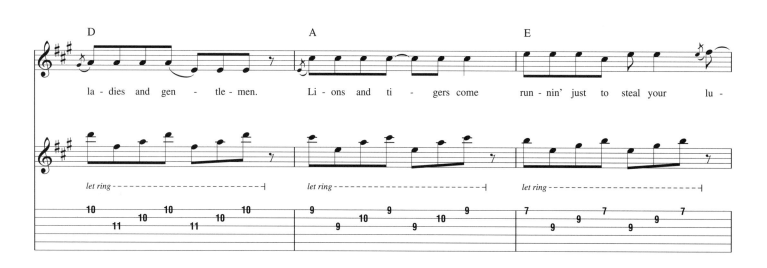

la - dies and gen - tle - men. Li - ons and ti - gers come run - nin' just to steal your lu -

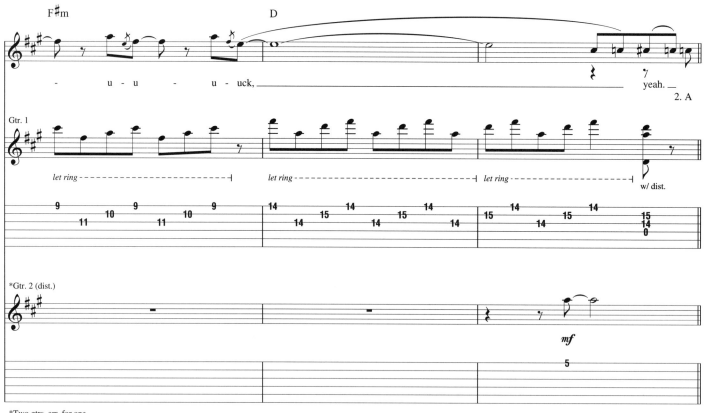

- u - u - u - uck, ___ yeah.

*Two gtrs. arr. for one.

Verse

rain-y Lith-u-a-ni-an who's danc-in' as an In-di-an. Paint-ed in my ti-ger skin, es-

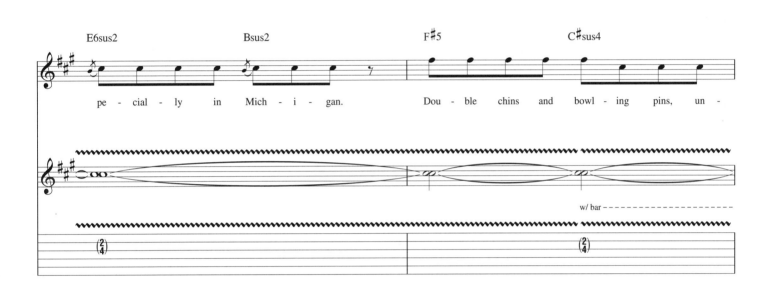

pe-cial-ly in Mich-i-gan. Dou-ble chins and bowl-ing pins, un-

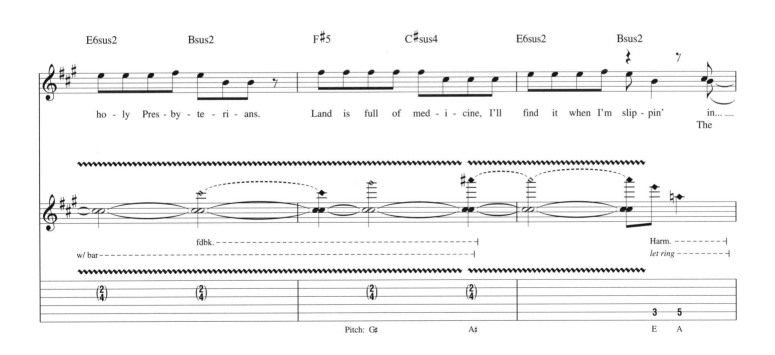

ho-ly Pres-by-te-ri-ans. Land is full of med-i-cine, I'll find it when I'm slip-pin' in... The

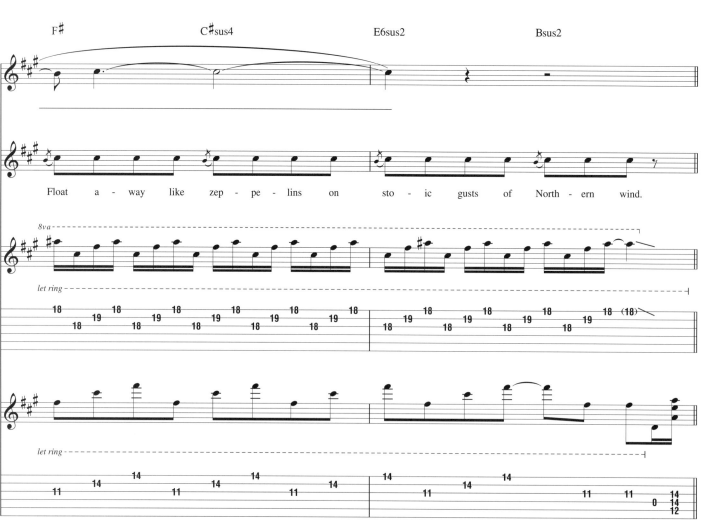

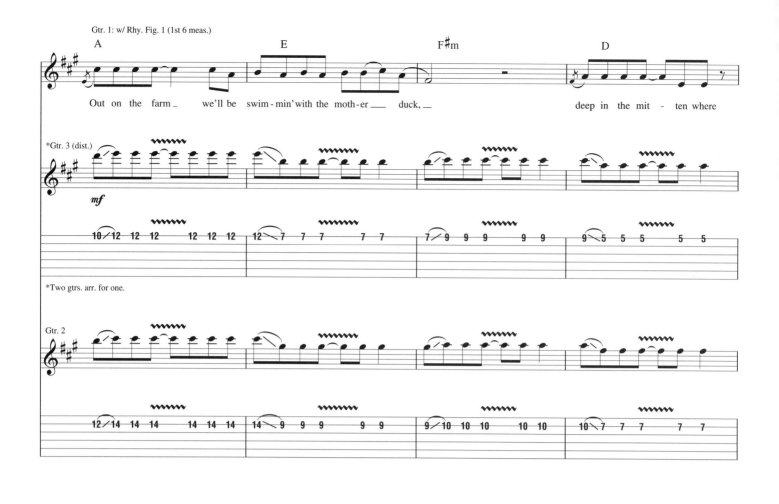

Out on the farm __ we'll be swim-min' with the moth-er __ duck, __ deep in the mit - ten where

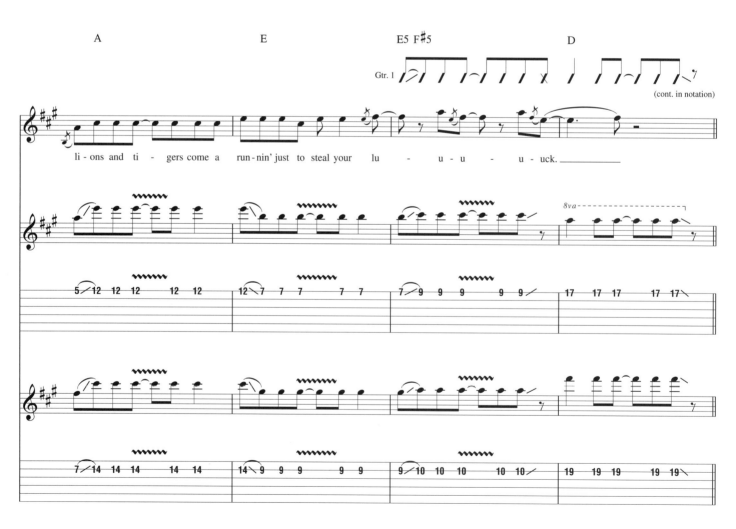

li - ons and ti - gers come a run-nin' just to steal your lu - u - u - u-uck. _____

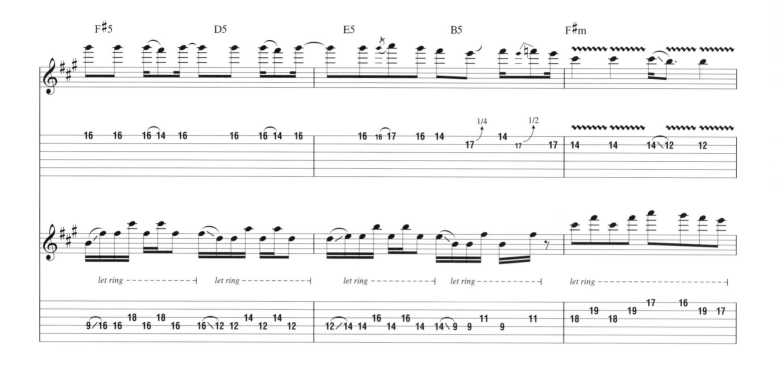

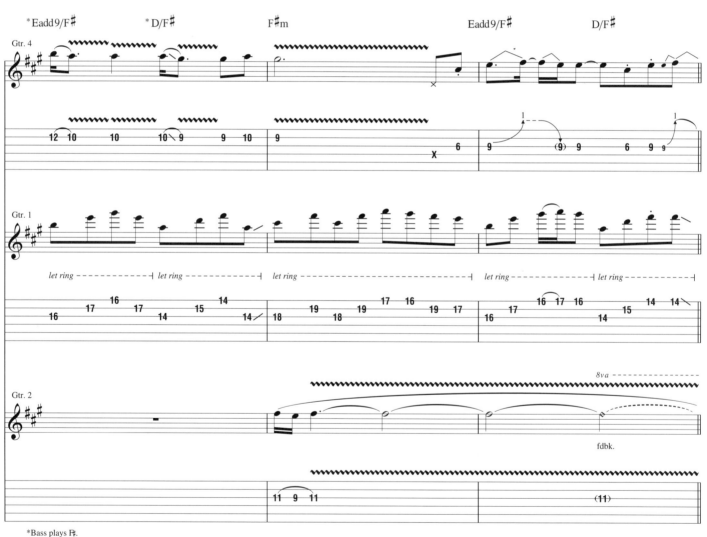

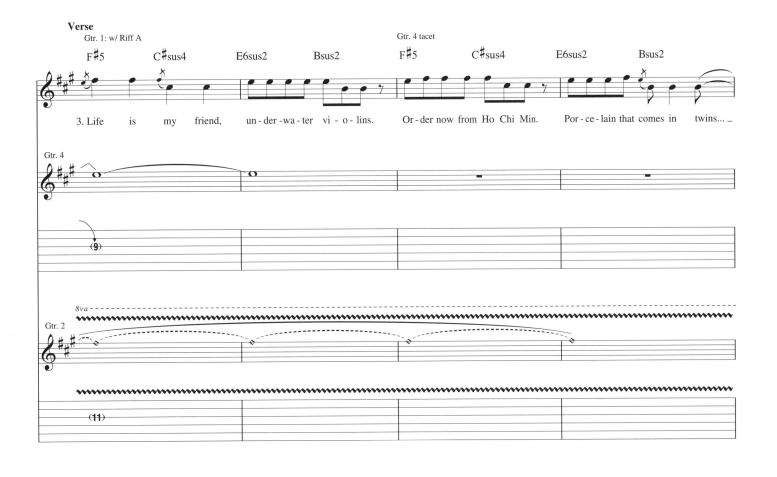

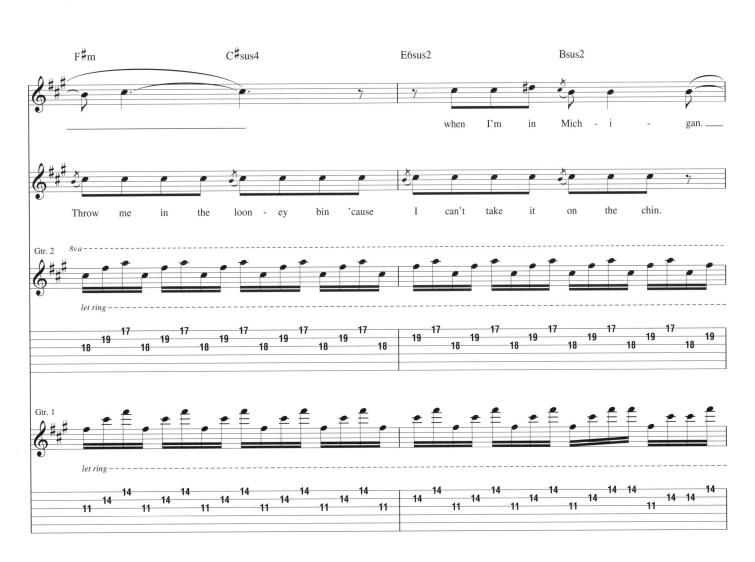

Chorus

Gtr. 1 tacet
Gtr. 3: w/ Rhy. Fig. 1 (1 3/4 times)

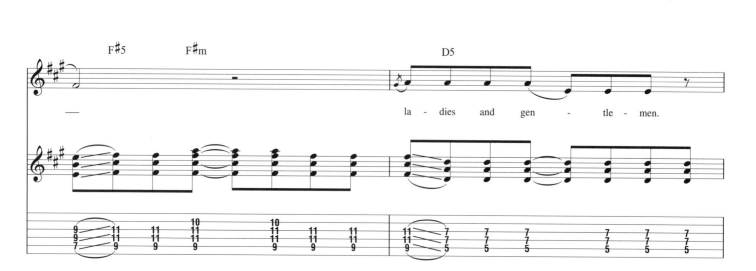

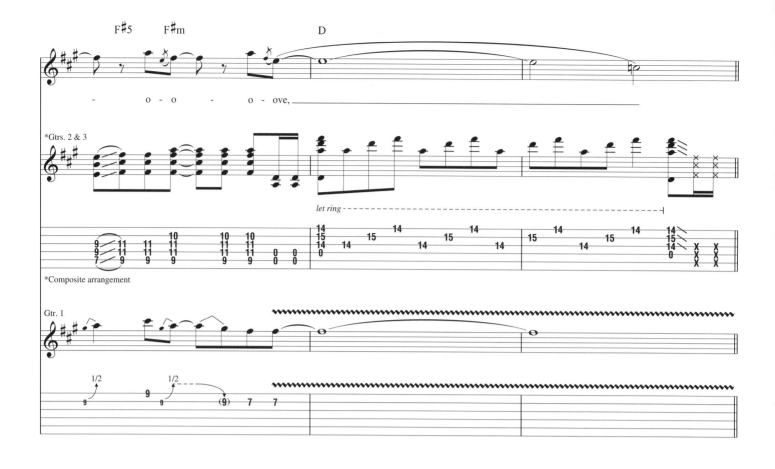

*Composite arrangement

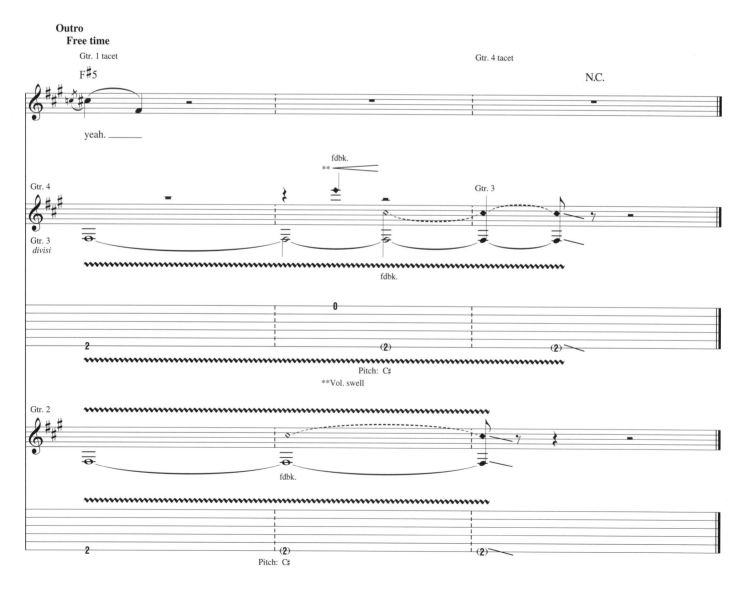

Warlocks

Words and Music by Anthony Kiedis, Flea, John Frusciante and Chad Smith

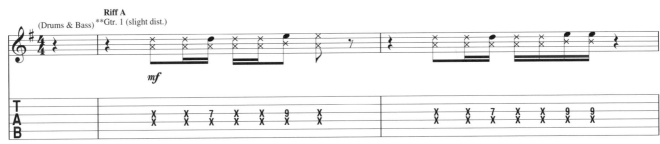

Intro
Moderately ♩ = 97

*Em7

*Chord symbols reflect implied harmony.
**Two gtrs. arr. for one.

End Riff A

% **Verse**

Gtr. 1: w/ Riff A (2 times)
2nd time, Gtrs. 2, 3, 4, 6 & 7 tacet
2nd time, Gtr. 5: w/ Fill 1

Em7

1. A, war-locks in won-der-land.__ I've got a,   a meg-a-trop-o-lis in__ my hand__ and a...
2. A, li-lacs and con-tra-band.__ I've got   San-ta Mon-i-ca in__ my hand. A lit-tle...

sub-ter-ra-ne-an march-ing__ band.__ I'm mak-in' noise for the boys in the Vat-i-can.   And a,
Beat-le ma-ni-a when__ I__ can.   I've got   two big bags of Old__ Ja-pan.__   Aw,

Fill 1
Gtr. 5

1 1/2
1

a lit - tle pack-age and off __ we go. __ Oh, tick - y, tick - y, tock - it - a, tic __ tac toe. I know...
ring - side, and blow __ by blow. An - oth - er... main e - vent at the old __ rain - bow. __ We're com - in'...

ev -'ry - bod - y is Es - kim - o. __ We got an - oth - er thing com - in', and that's __ our show, __ well,
right on top of the tu - pe - lo, __ a when she looks a just like Bri - gitte __ Bar - dot. __

Chorus

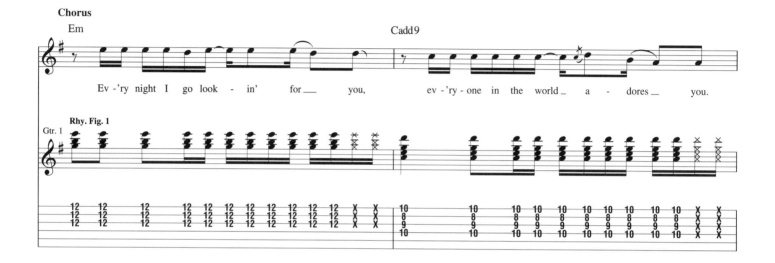

Ev -'ry night I go look - in' for __ you, ev -'ry - one in the world __ a - dores __ you.

Rhy. Fig. 1

Gtr. 1

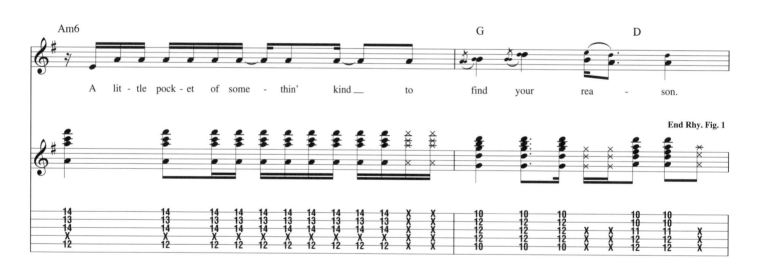

A lit - tle pock - et of some - thin' kind __ to find your rea - son.

End Rhy. Fig. 1

Gtr. 1: w/ Rhy. Fig. 1

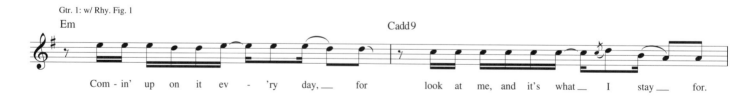

Com - in' up on it ev -'ry day, __ for look at me, and it's what __ I stay __ for.

To Coda

A lit - tle lock - et of fan - ta - sy __ that we be - lieve __ in.

Interlude

Em7

Gtr. 6
(slight dist.)

Gtr. 7 (slight dist.)
divisi

**w/ delay

mf

**w/ delay

steady gliss.

steady gliss.

**Set for sixteenth-note regeneration w/ one repeat.

Gtr. 5 (slight dist.)

mf grad. release

grad. bend

grad. release

grad. bend

Gtr. 4 (slight dist.)
divisi

mf grad. release

grad. release

***

***Gtr. 5 to the left of slashes in tab.

*w/ delay

mf

Gtr. 2
(slight dist.)

Gtr. 3
(slight dist.)
divisi

mf
*w/ delay

*Set for sixteenth-note regeneration w/ one repeat.

⊕ Coda

Interlude

Gtr. 1: w/ Riff A

Em7

Bridge

Cadd9

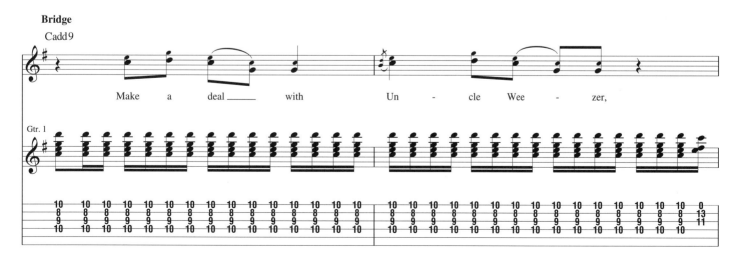

Make a deal _____ with Un - cle Wee - zer,

Gtr. 1

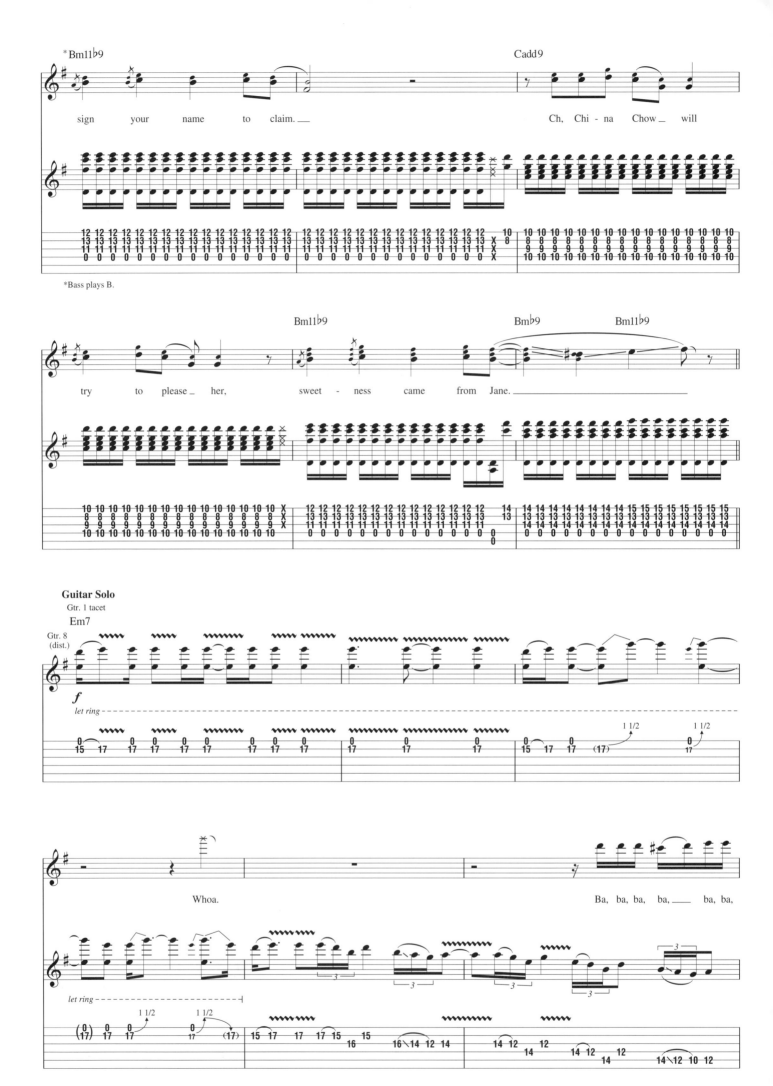

*Bass plays B.

Guitar Solo
Gtr. 1 tacet

C'mon Girl

Words and Music by Anthony Kiedis, Flea, John Frusciante and Chad Smith

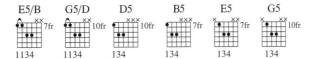

*Two gtrs. arr. for one.

**Chord symbols reflect implied harmony.

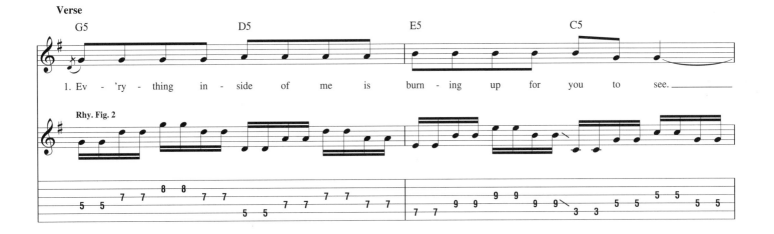

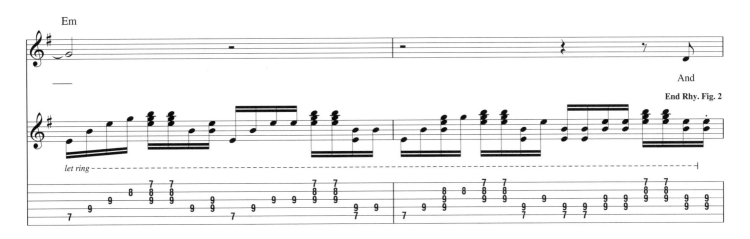

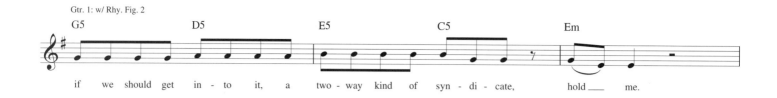

Gtr. 1: w/ Rhy. Fig. 2

G5　　　　　　D5　　　　　　E5　　　　　C5　　　　　　Em

if we should get in - to it, a two-way kind of syn - di - cate, hold __ me.

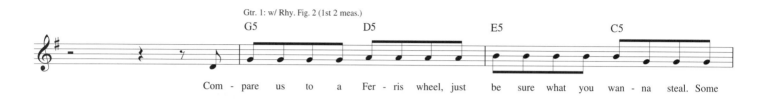

Gtr. 1: w/ Rhy. Fig. 2 (1st 2 meas.)

G5　　　　　　D5　　　　　　E5　　　　　C5

Com - pare us to a Fer - ris wheel, just be sure what you wan - na steal. Some

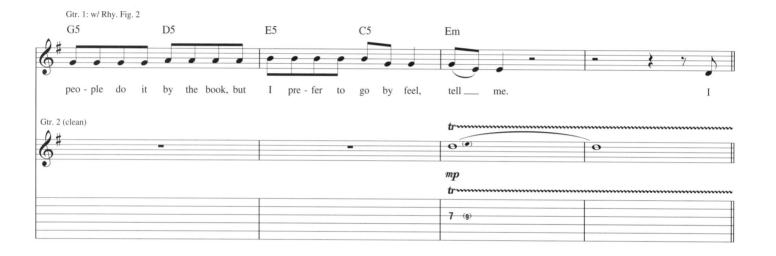

Gtr. 1: w/ Rhy. Fig. 2

G5　　　　　　D5　　　　　　E5　　C5　　　Em

peo - ple do it by the book, but I pre - fer to go by feel, tell __ me.　　　　　I

Gtr. 2 (clean)

mp

Pre-Chorus

Gtr. 2 tacet

Am　　　　　　　　C　　　　　　　　G　　　　　　　　D

want - ed to get out - ta here, but ev - 'ry time I re - ap - pear.

Rhy. Fig. 3

Gtr. 1

let ring ----------　*let ring ----------*　*let ring ----------*　*let ring ----------*

Am　　　　　　　　C　　　　　　　　G　　　　　　　　D

Now I have the words, my dear, to whis - per right in - to your ear,

let ring ----------　*let ring ----------*　*let ring ----------*　*let ring ----------*

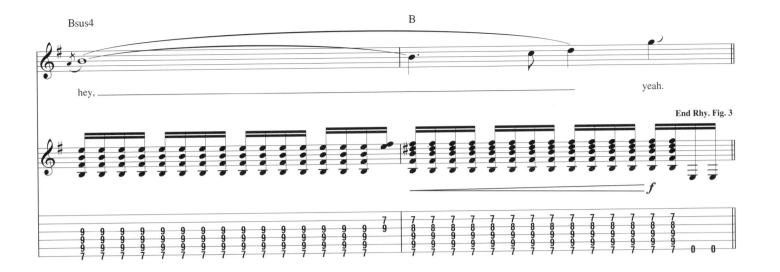

Bsus4   B

hey, _____ yeah.

End Rhy. Fig. 3

Chorus

E5   G5   D5   B5   D5   E5   G5   D5   B5

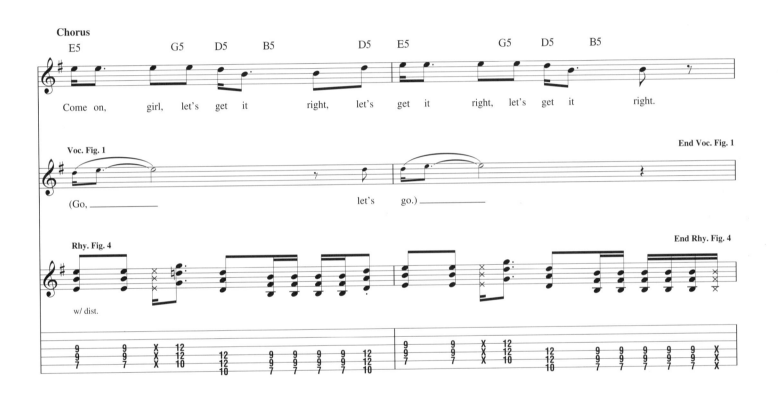

Come on,   girl, let's get it   right,   let's   get it   right, let's   get   it   right.

Voc. Fig. 1

End Voc. Fig. 1

(Go, _____ let's   go.) _____

Rhy. Fig. 4

End Rhy. Fig. 4

w/ dist.

Bkgd. Voc.: w/ Voc. Fig. 1 (3 times)
Gtr. 1: w/ Rhy. Fig. 4 (3 times)

E5   G5   D5   B5   D5   E5   G5   D5   B5   E5   G5   D5   B5   D5

Come on,   girl, let's get it   right, let's   get it   right, let's   get it   right.   Come on,   girl, let's   get it   right,   let's

E5   G5   D5   B5   D5   E5   G5   D5   B5   D5   E5   G5   D5   B5

get it   right, let's   get it   right.   Come on,   girl, let's   get it   right,   let's   get it   right, let's   get it   right.

Interlude

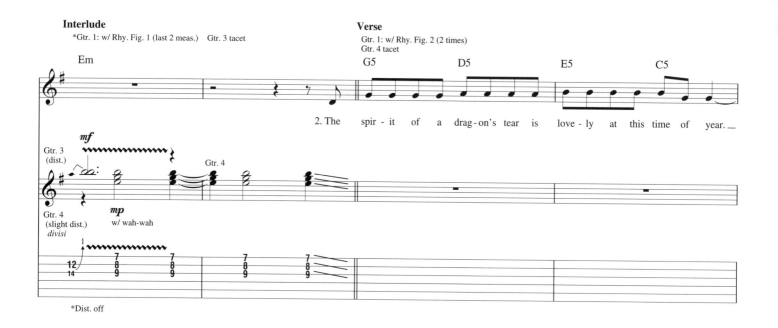

Verse

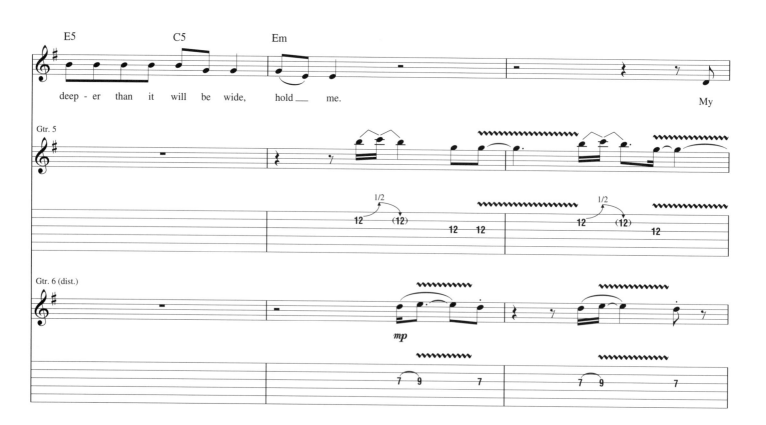

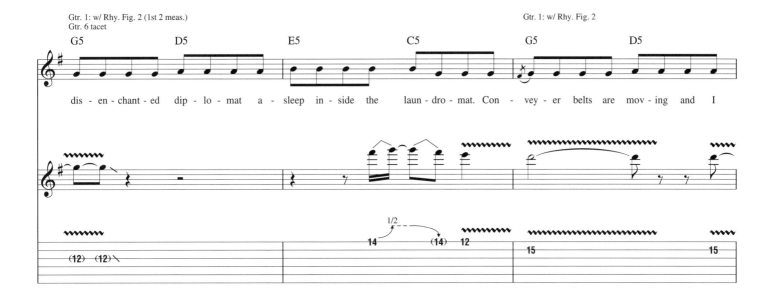

Pre-Chorus

if you let it ger - mi - nate I know it will be worth the wait. Dis - put - ed by the news that it was

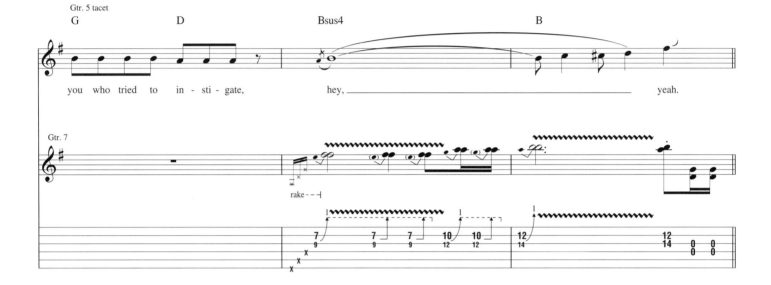

you who tried to in - sti - gate, hey, yeah.

Chorus

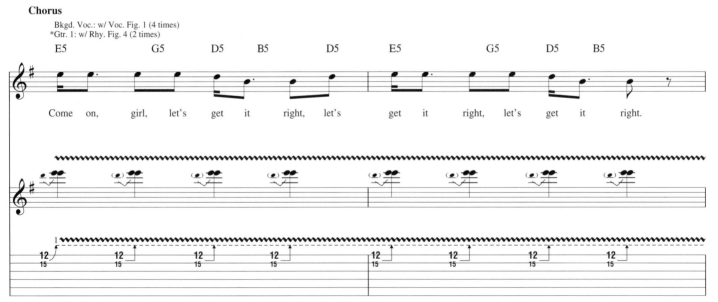

Come on, girl, let's get it right, let's get it right, let's get it right.

Interlude

*Gtr. 1: w/ Rhy. Fig. 1
Gtr. 7 tacet

Pre-Chorus

Bless-ed are the hyp-o-crites, out-wit-ted, but she nev-er quits. The trou-ble with a band of slits is wash-ing off the mud-dy bits,

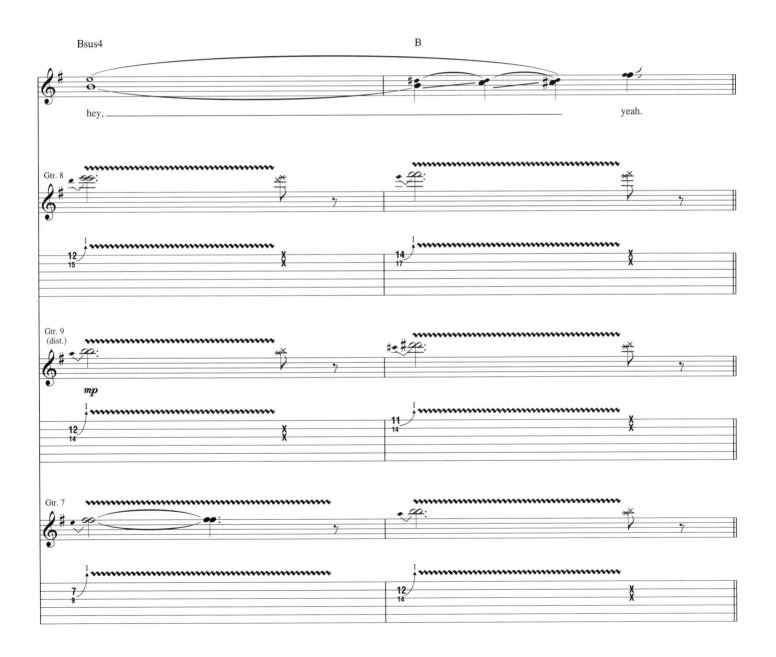

hey, _____ yeah.

Outro-Guitar Solo

Gtrs. 8 & 9 tacet

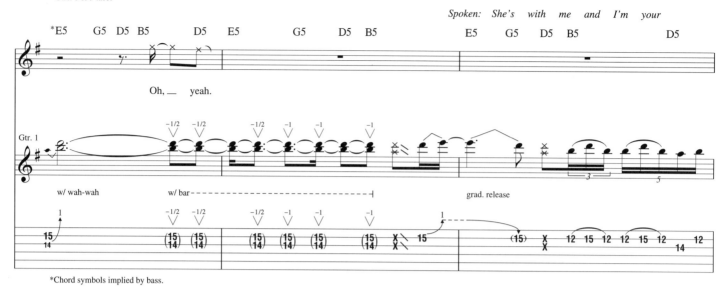

*Chord symbols implied by bass.

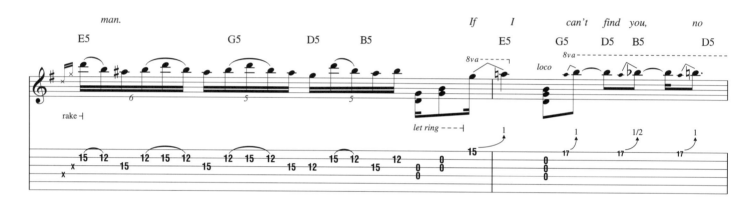

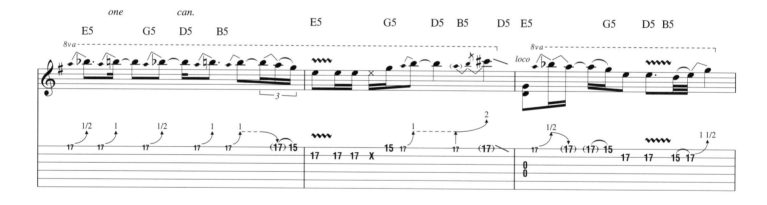

Free time

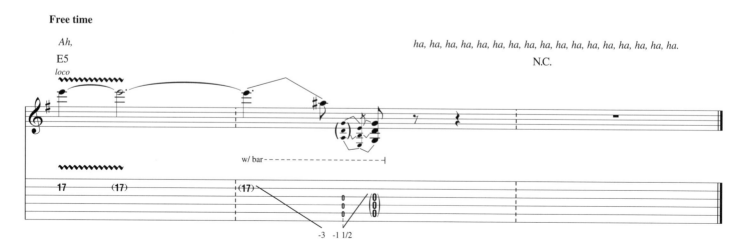

112

Wet Sand

Words and Music by Anthony Kiedis, Flea, John Frusciante and Chad Smith

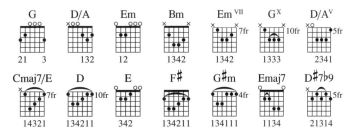

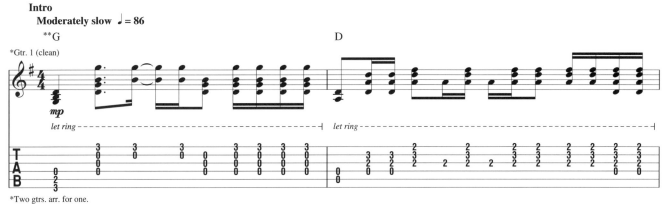

*Two gtrs. arr. for one.

**Chord symbols reflect implied harmony.

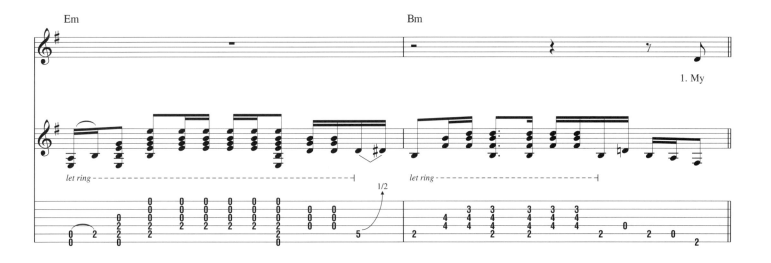

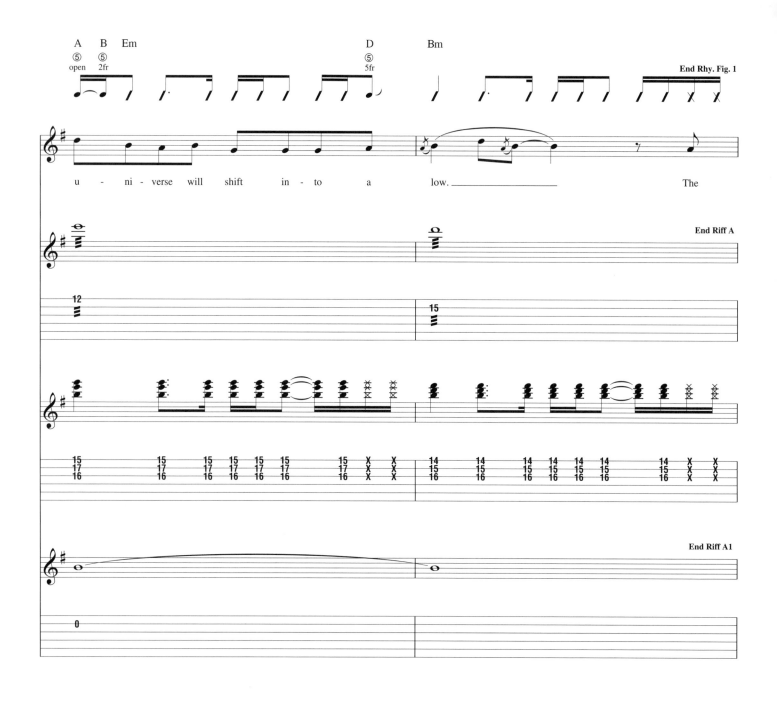

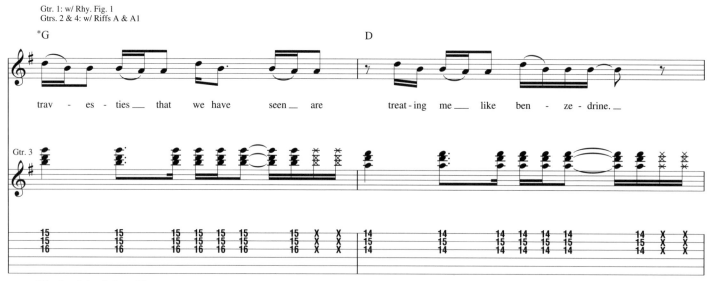

*Chord symbols reflect overall harmony.

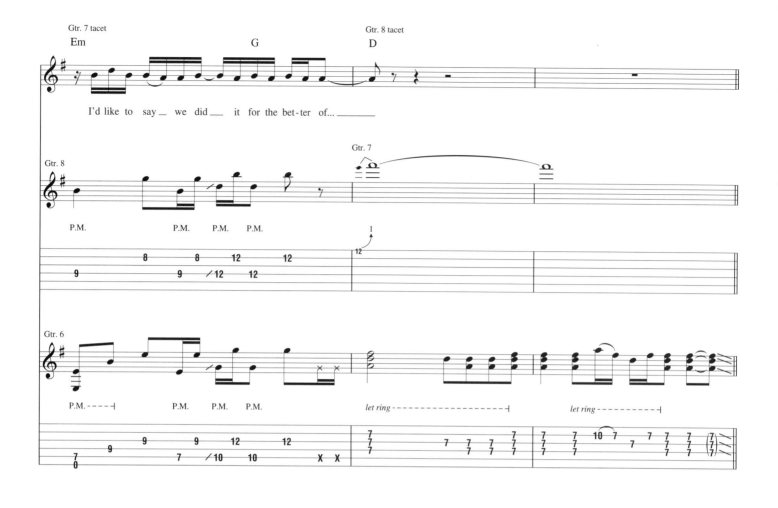

I'd like to say ___ we did ___ it for the bet-ter of... ___

Chorus

I thought a - bout it and I brought it ___ out. ___

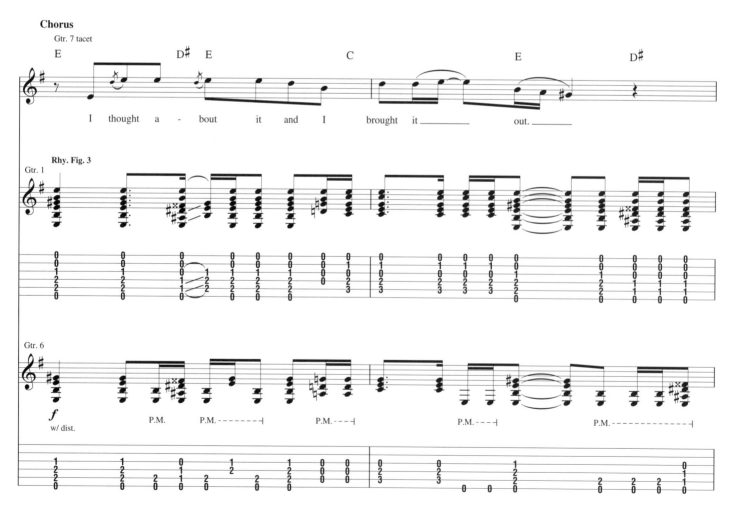

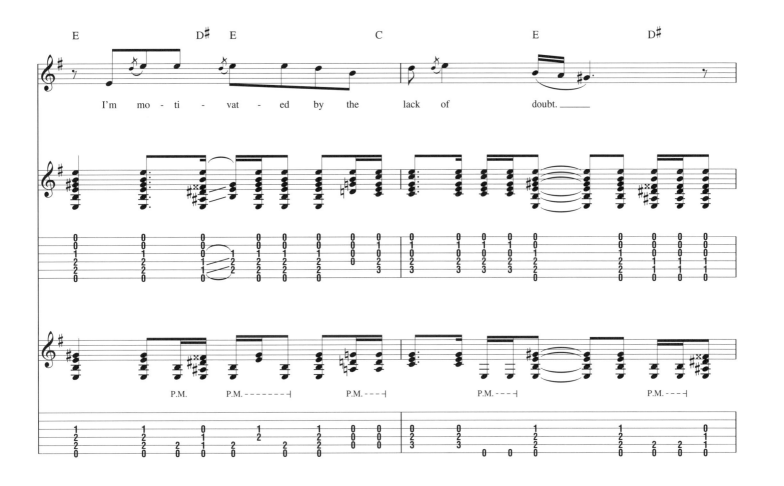

I'm mo-ti-vat-ed by the lack of doubt. _____

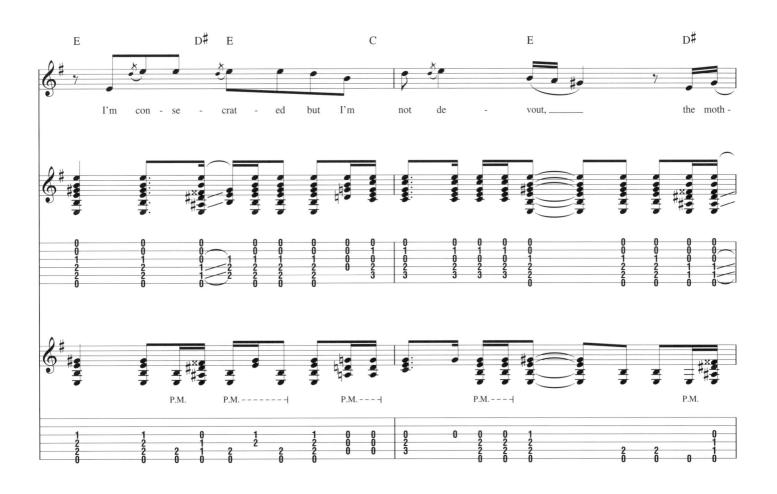

I'm con-se-crat-ed but I'm not de-vout, _____ the moth-

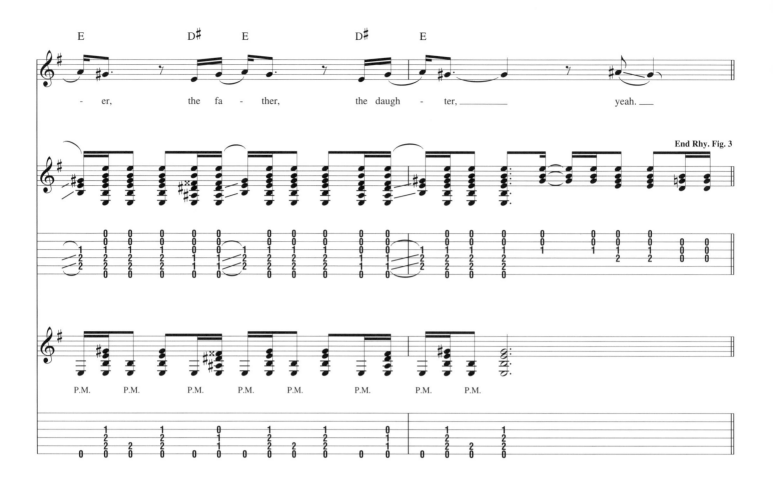

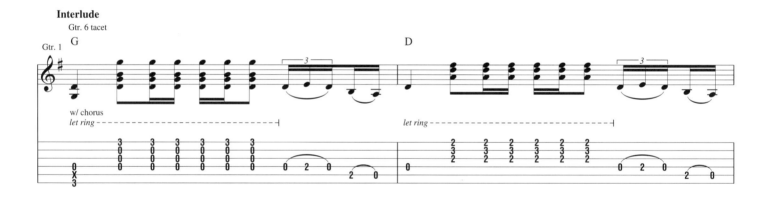

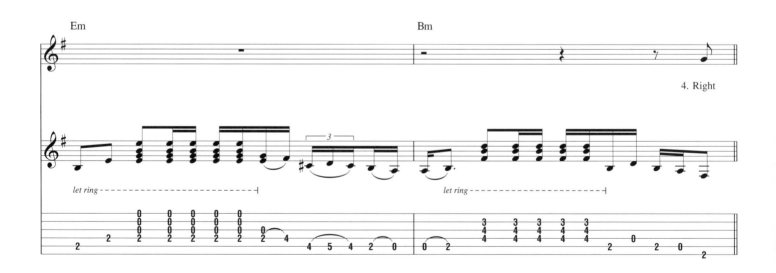

Verse

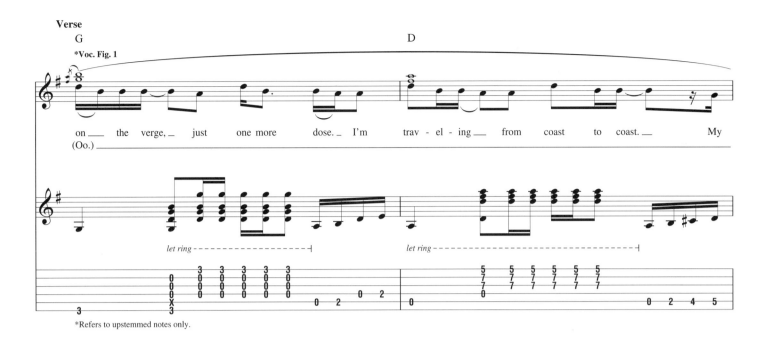

*Refers to upstemmed notes only.

on ___ the verge, ___ just one more dose. ___ I'm trav-el-ing ___ from coast to coast. ___ My
(Oo.) _____

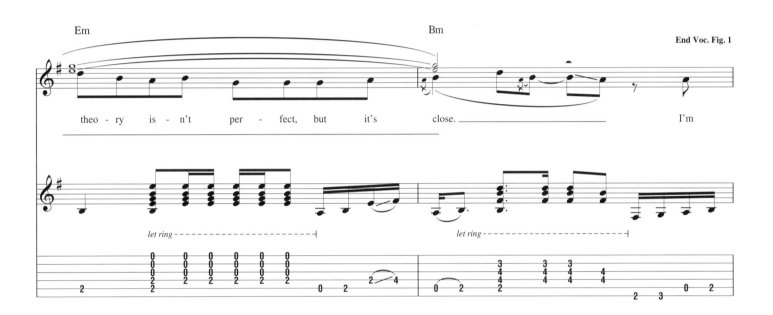

theo - ry is - n't per - fect, but it's close. _____ I'm

End Voc. Fig. 1

Bkgd. Voc.: w/ Voc. Fig. 1

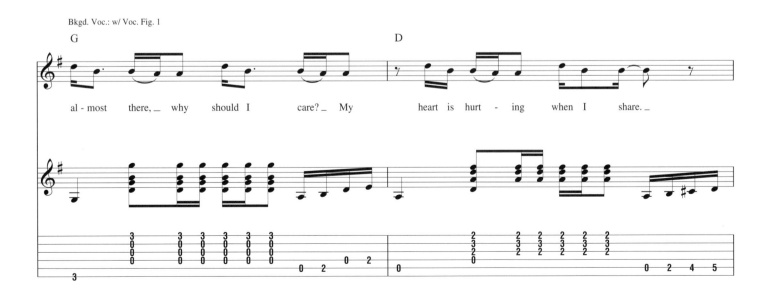

al - most there, ___ why should I care? My heart is hurt - ing when I share. ___

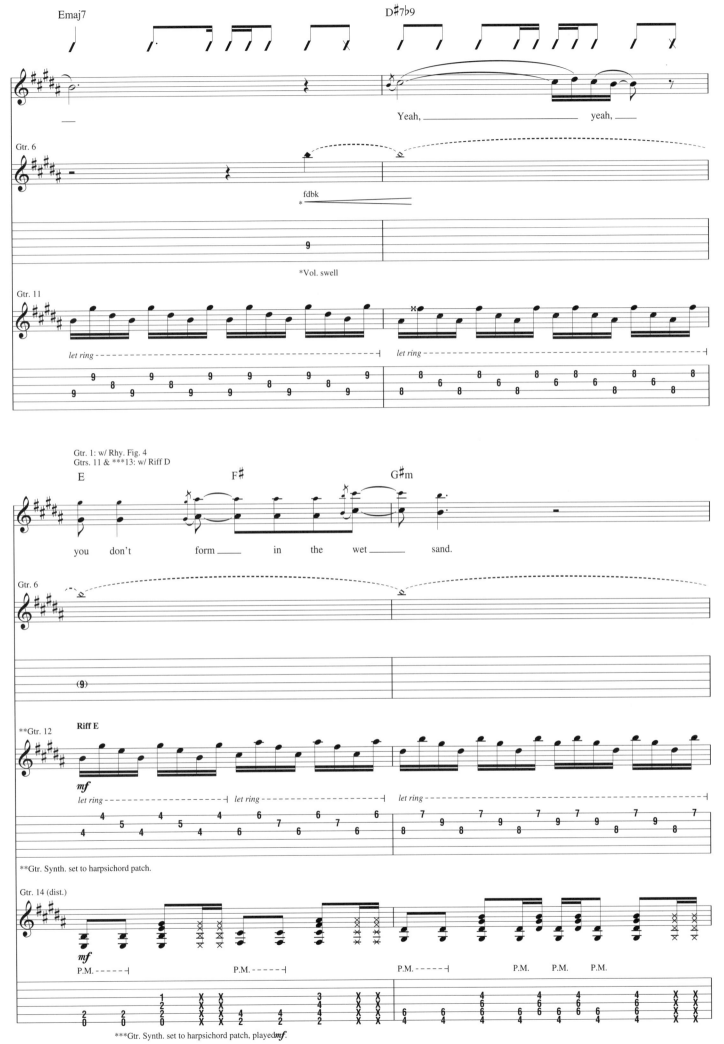

*Composite arrangement
**Composite arrangement

Outro-Guitar Solo

Gtrs. 1 & 14: w/ Rhy. Fig. 4
Gtr. 6 tacet
Gtrs. 11 & 13: w/ Riff D
Gtr. 12: w/ Riff E

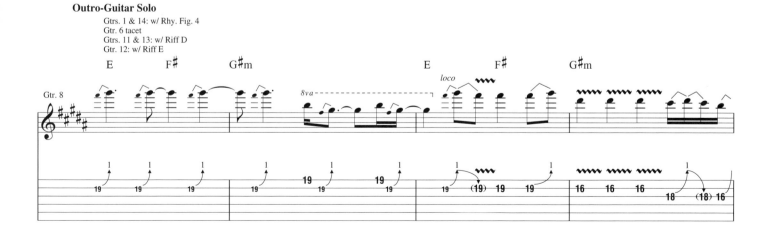

Hey

Words and Music by Anthony Kiedis, Flea, John Frusciante and Chad Smith

Intro
Moderately fast ♩ = 122

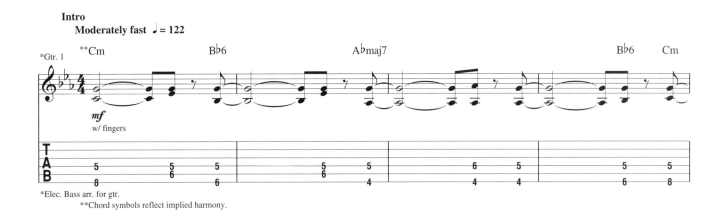

*Elec. Bass arr. for gtr.
**Chord symbols reflect implied harmony.

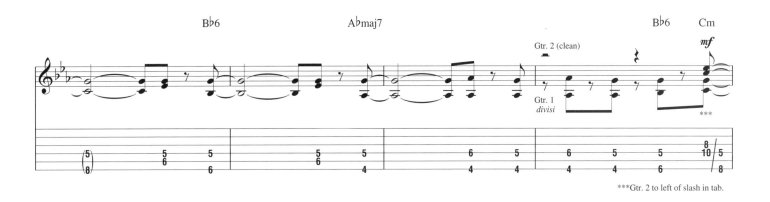

***Gtr. 2 to left of slash in tab.

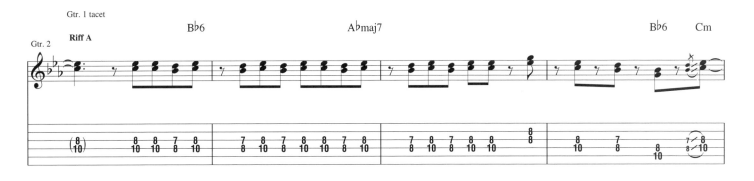

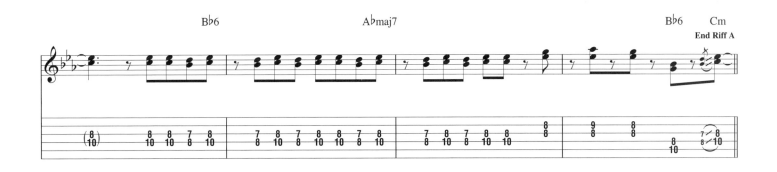

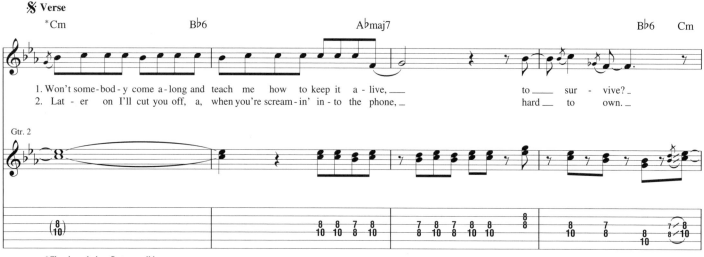

1. Won't some-bod-y come a-long and teach me how to keep it a-live, ___ to ___ sur - vive?
2. Lat - er on I'll cut you off, a, when you're scream-in' in-to the phone, _ hard _ to own. _

*Chord symbols reflect overall harmony.

Come a - long and show me some-thing that I nev - er knew in your eyes. _ Take _ a - way the tour - ni - quet.
An - y - way, I wan - na let .you know that ev -'ry-thing is on hold. _ What _ you gon - na do to me?

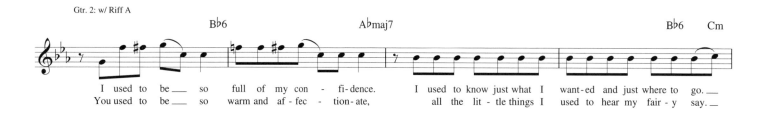

I used to be ___ so full of my con - fi - dence. I used to know just what I want-ed and just where to go. ___
You used to be ___ so warm and af - fec - tion-ate, all the lit - tle things I used to hear my fair - y say. ___

To Coda ⊕

A, more than ev - er, I could use a co - in - ci - dence, but now I walk a - lone and talk a - bout it, when I know.
But now you're quick _ to get in - to your _ re - gret. I'll take a fall and now you got to give it all a - way.

Chorus

Gtr. 2: w/ Riff A (1st 4 meas.)

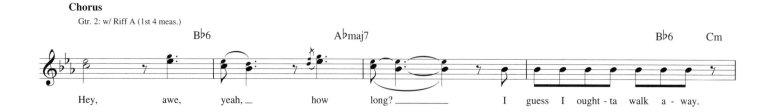

Hey, awe, yeah, _ how long? ___ I guess I ought - ta walk a - way.

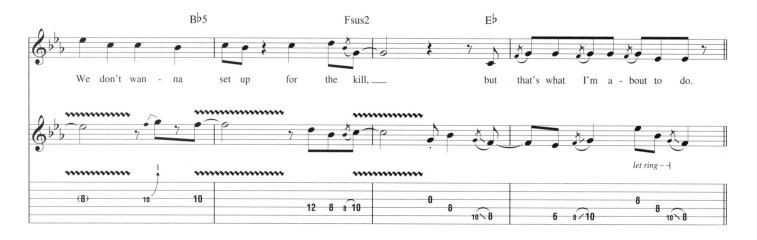

We don't wan - na   set up   for   the   kill, ___   but   that's what   I'm a - bout to   do.

let ring ⌐

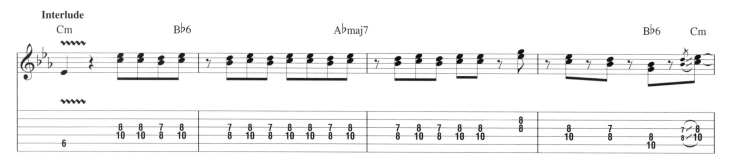

Interlude

Cm   Bb6   Abmaj7   Bb6   Cm

D.S. al Coda

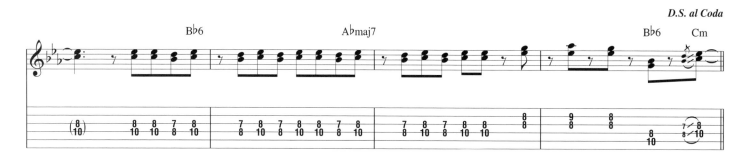

Bb6   Abmaj7   Bb6   Cm

 Coda

Chorus

Gtr. 2: w/ Riff A (1st 4 meas.)

Bb6   Abmaj7

Hey,   awe,   yeah, ___   how

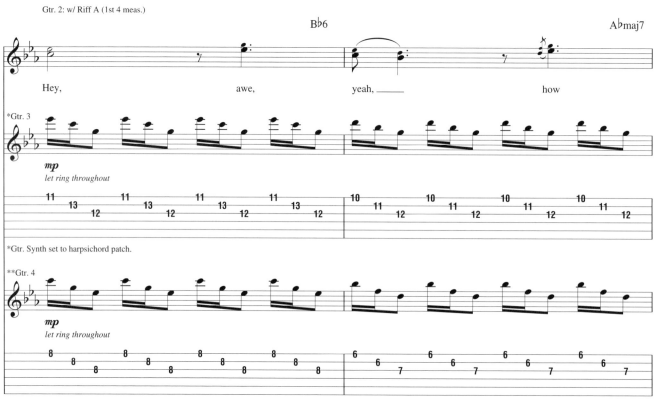

*Gtr. 3

mp

let ring throughout

*Gtr. Synth set to harpsichord patch.

**Gtr. 4

mp

let ring throughout

**Gtr. Synth set to harpsichord patch.

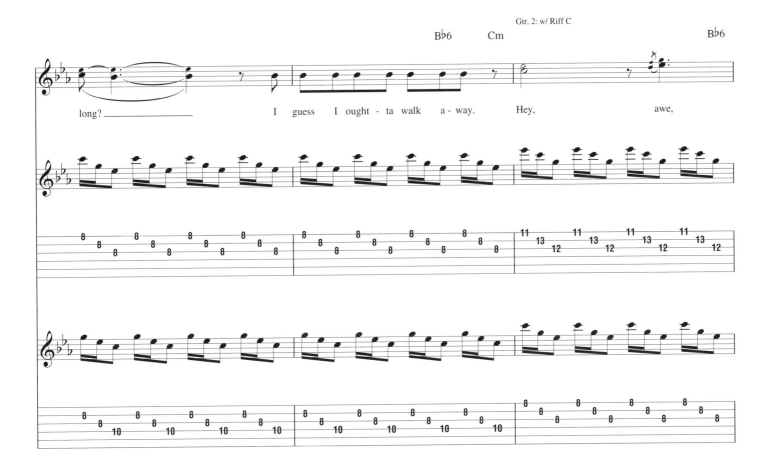

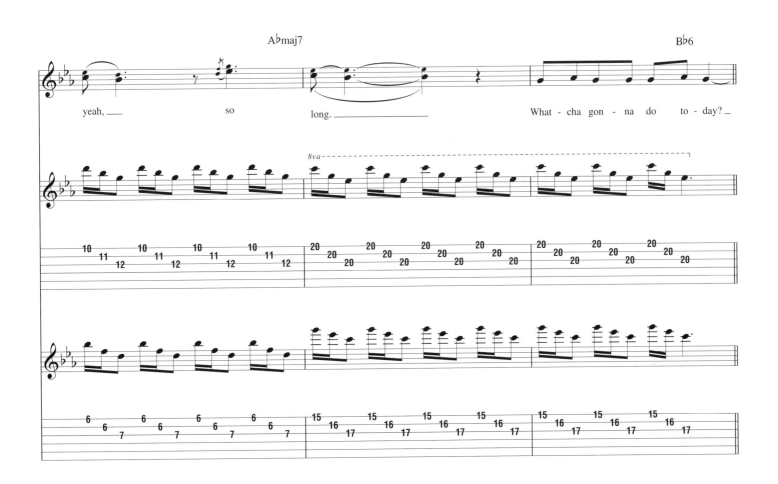

Interlude

Gtrs. 3 & 4 tacet

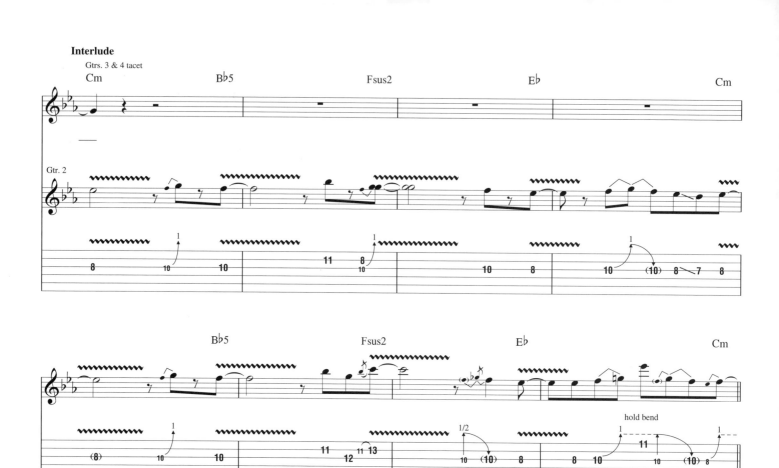

Bridge

I don't wan - na have to but I will, ____ if that's what I'm sup - posed to do.

We don't wan - na set up for the kill, ____ but that's what I'm a - bout to do.

Guitar Solo

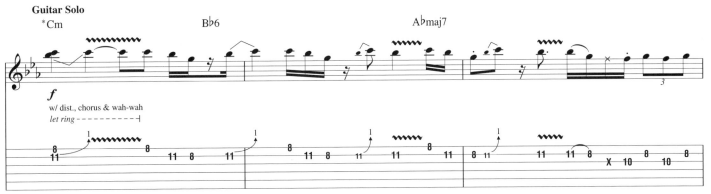

*Chord symbols implied by bass, next 16 meas.

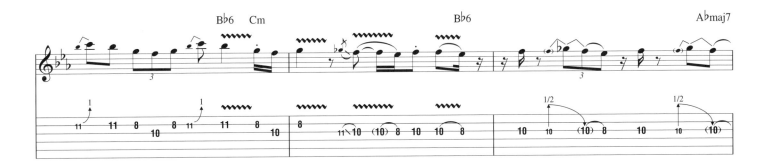

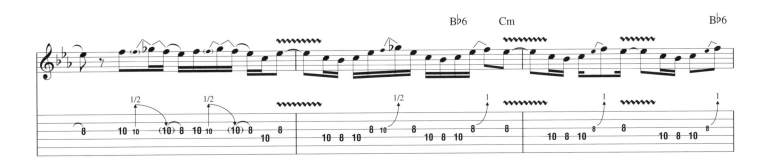

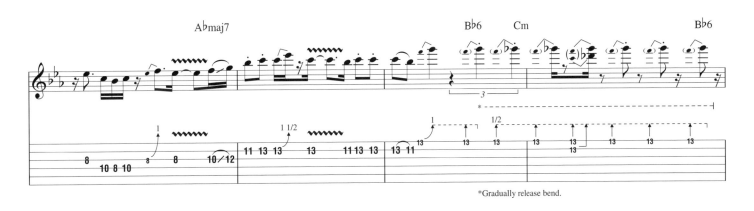

*Gradually release bend.

Desecration Smile

Words and Music by Anthony Kiedis, Flea, John Frusciante and Chad Smith

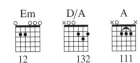

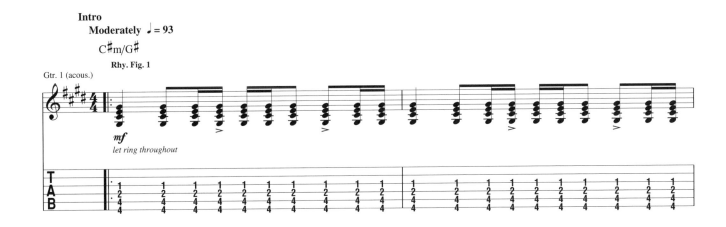

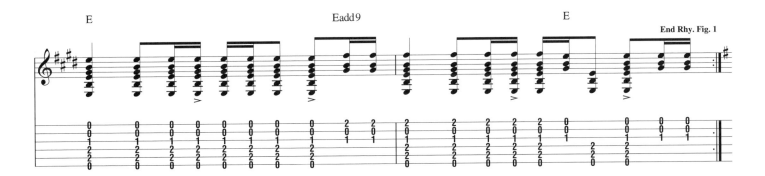

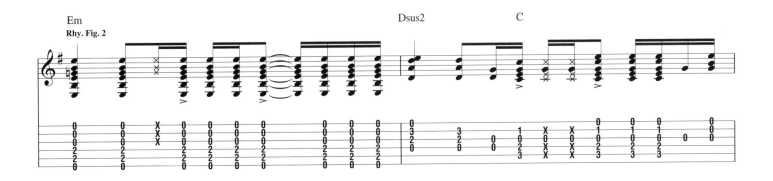

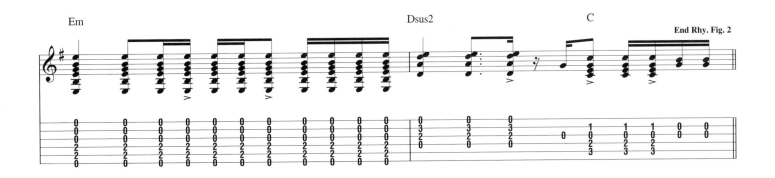

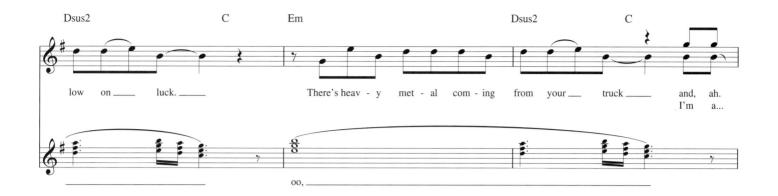

Dsus2   C   Em   Dsus2   C

low on   luck.   There's heav - y met - al com - ing from your   truck   and, ah.
                                                                                I'm a...

oo,

D.S. al Coda 1

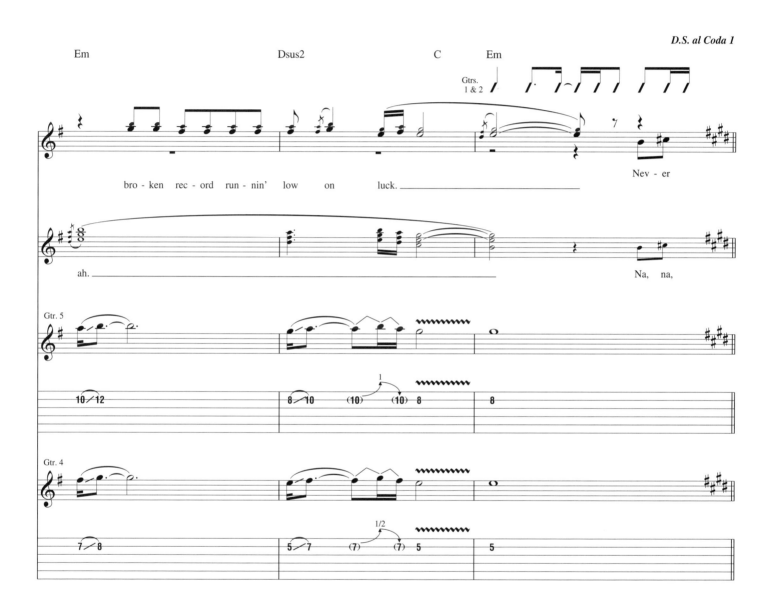

Em   Dsus2   C   Em

Gtrs.
1 & 2

bro - ken rec - ord run - nin' low on luck.   Nev - er

ah.   Na, na,

Gtr. 5

10/12   8/10   (10)   (10) 8   8

Gtr. 4

7/8   5/7   (7)   (7) 5   5

$\oplus$ **Coda 1**

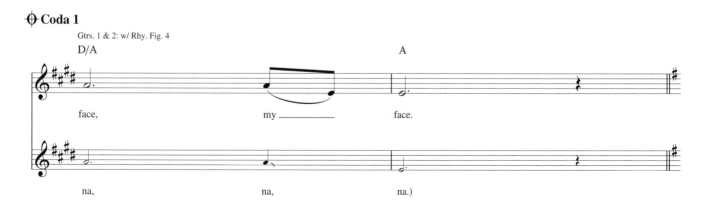

Gtrs. 1 & 2: w/ Rhy. Fig. 4

D/A   A

face,   my   face.

na,   na,   na.)

Interlude

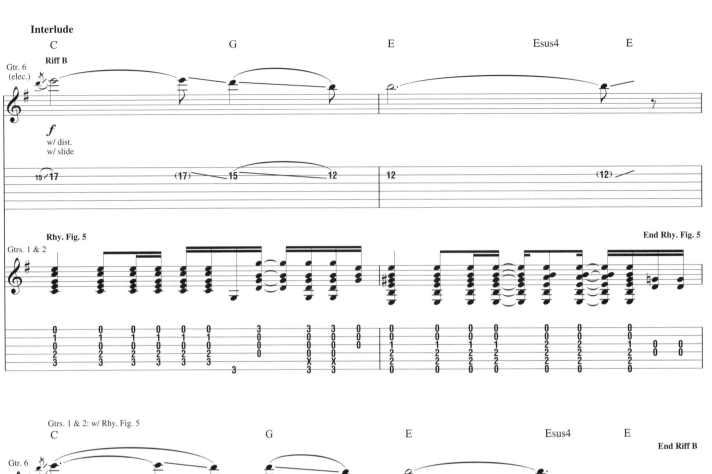

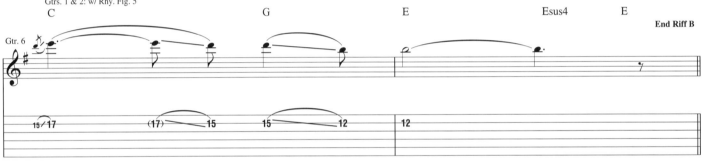

Bridge

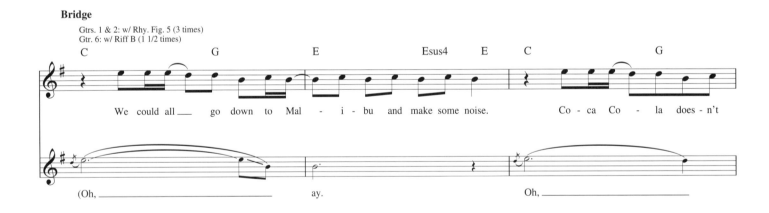

We could all ___ go down to Mal - i - bu and make some noise. Co - ca Co - la does - n't

(Oh, _____ ay. Oh, _____

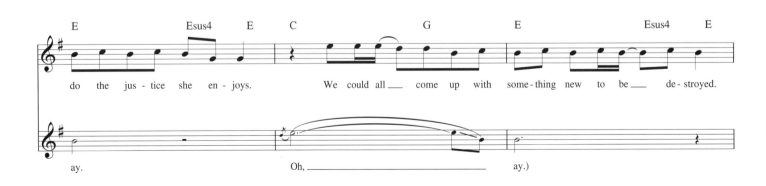

do the jus - tice she en - joys. We could all ___ come up with some - thing new to be ___ de - stroyed.

ay. Oh, _____ ay.)

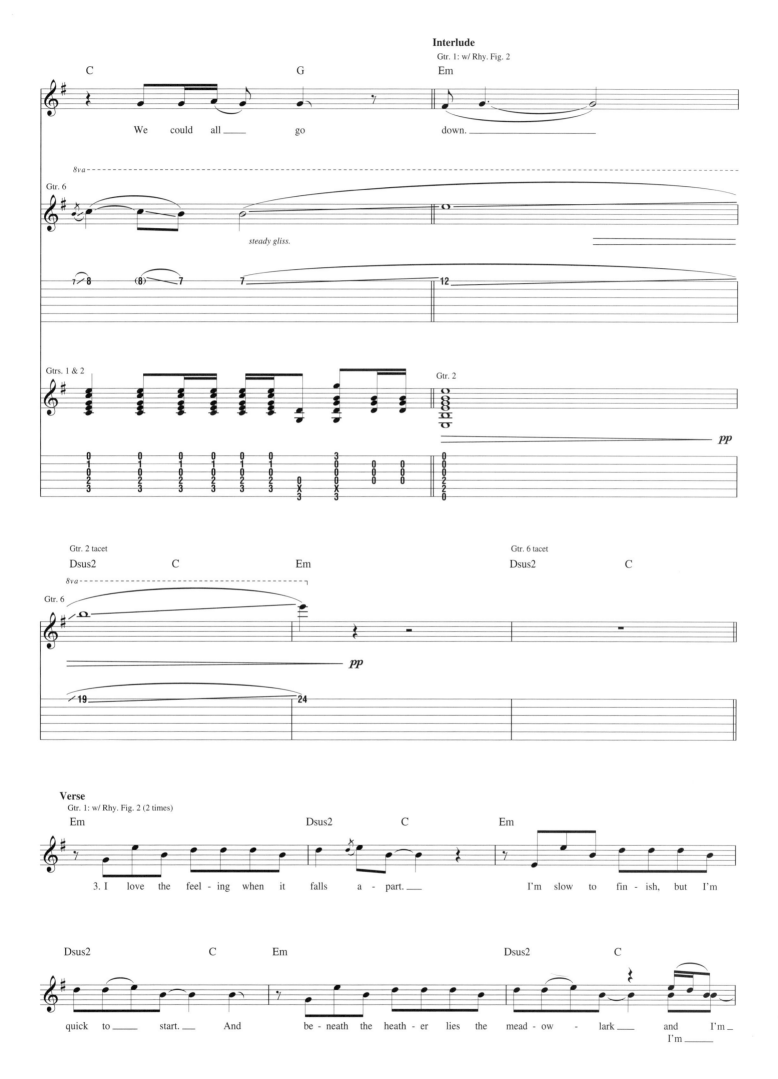

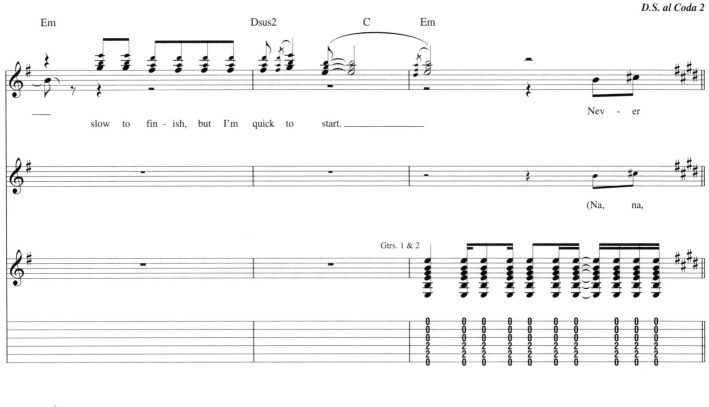

Coda 2

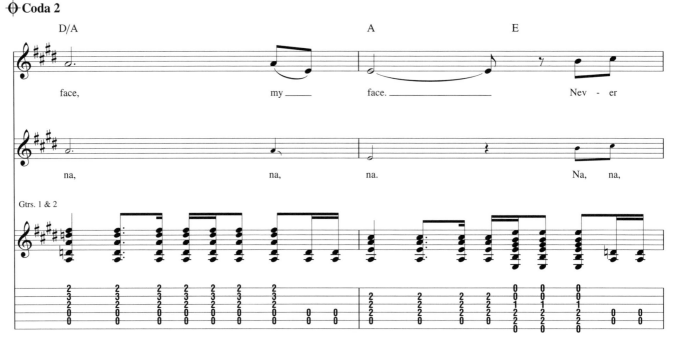

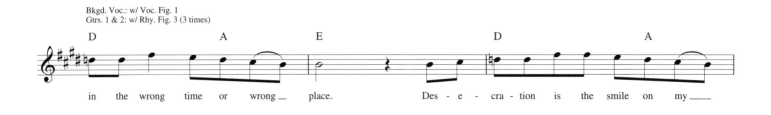

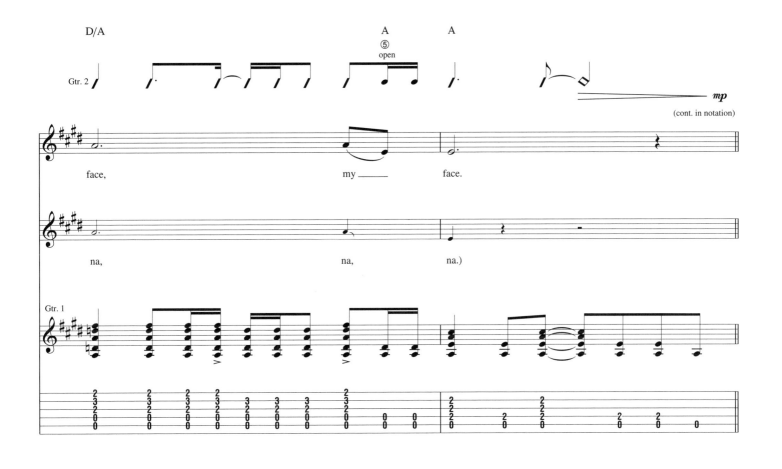

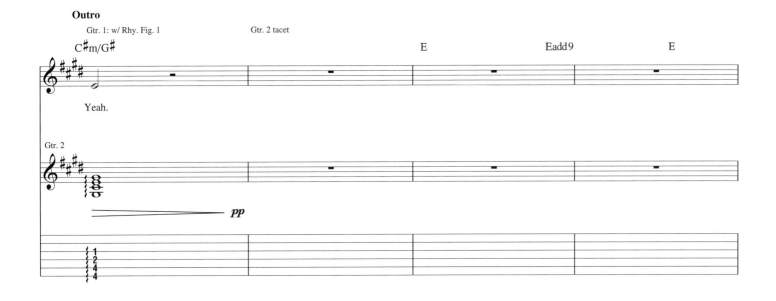

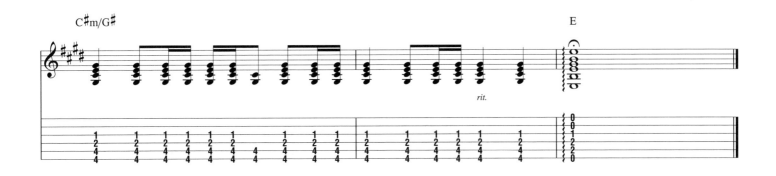

Tell Me Baby

Words and Music by Anthony Kiedis, Flea, John Frusciante and Chad Smith

*Chord symbols reflect implied harmony.

*2nd time, w/ fast, heavy phase shifter

1. They come from ev - 'ry state __ to find __ some dreams were meant to be __ de - clined.
2. Some claim to have the for - ti - tude too shrewd to blow the in - ter - lude,

Tell the man, what did you have __ in mind? What have you come to do?
sus - tain - ing pain to set __ a mood, step out to be re - newed.

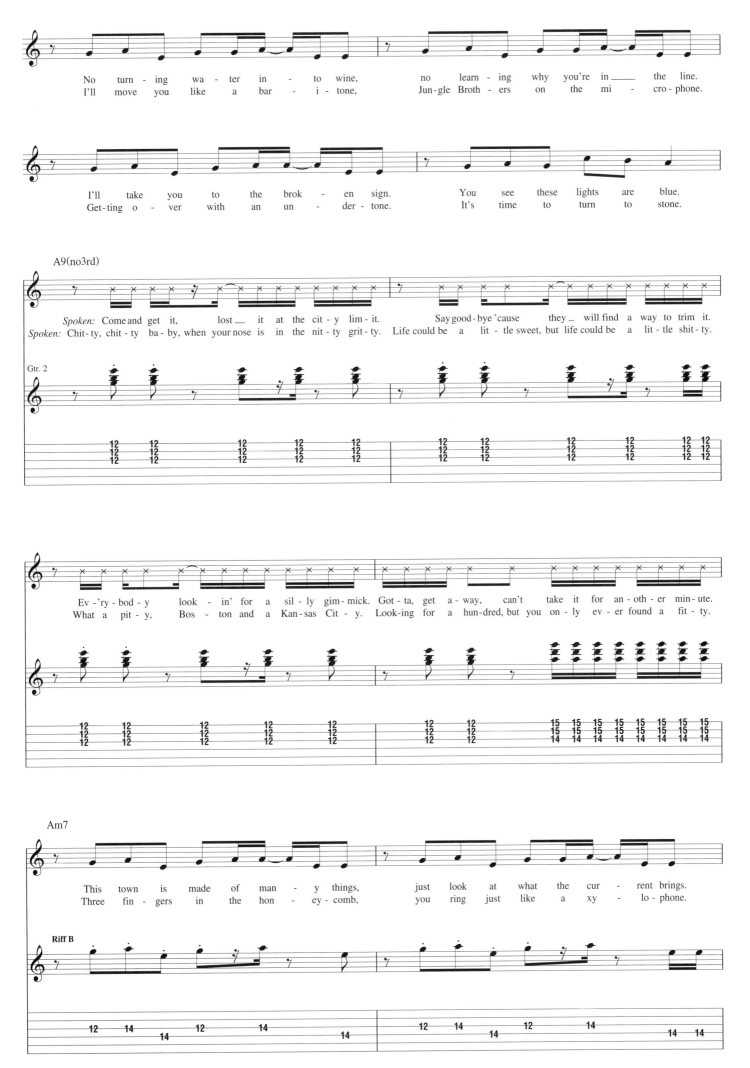

D.S. al Coda

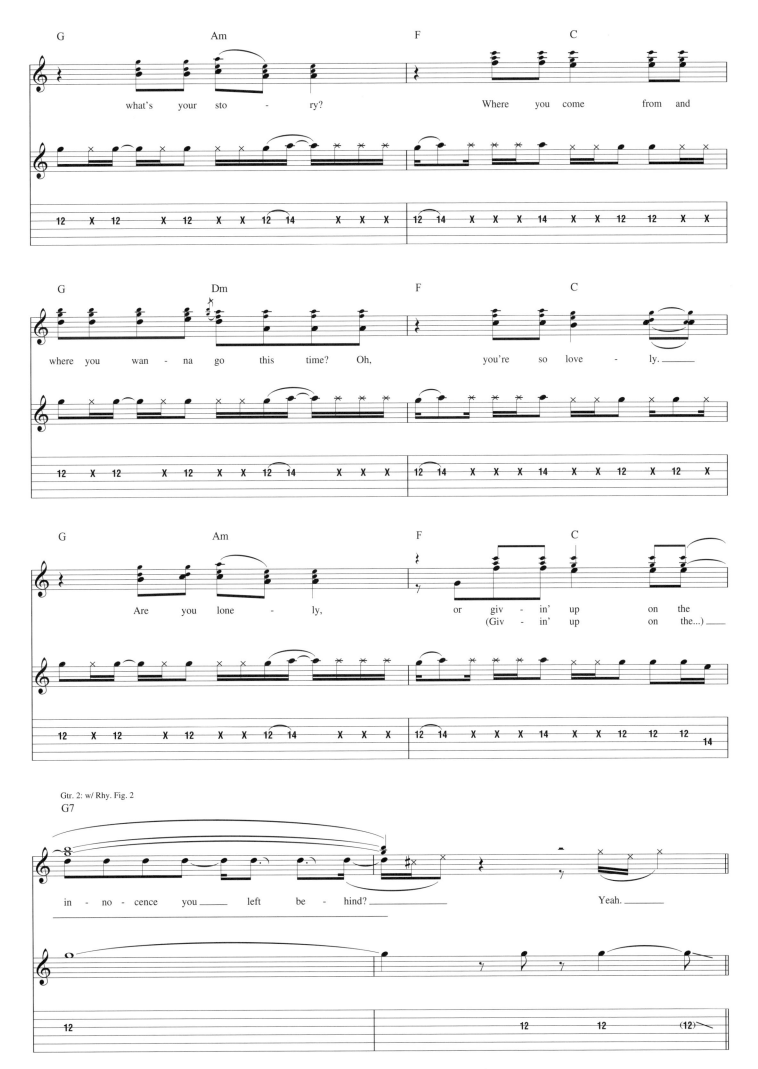

Guitar Solo

Hard to Concentrate

Words and Music by Anthony Kiedis, Flea, John Frusciante and Chad Smith

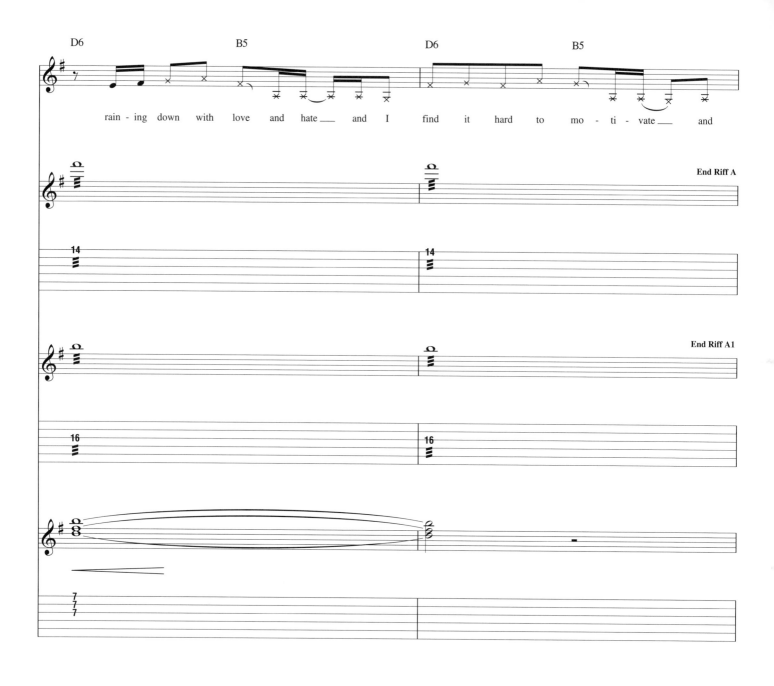

rain - ing down with love and hate ___ and I find it hard to mo - ti - vate ___ and

Gtrs. 2 & 3: w/ Riffs A & A1

es - tu - ar - y ___ is blessed ___ but scar - y. ___ Your

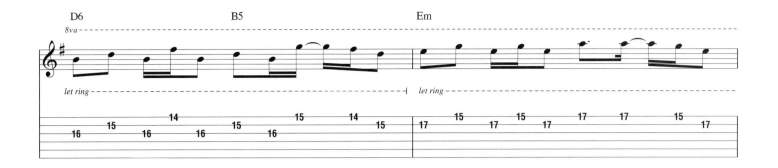

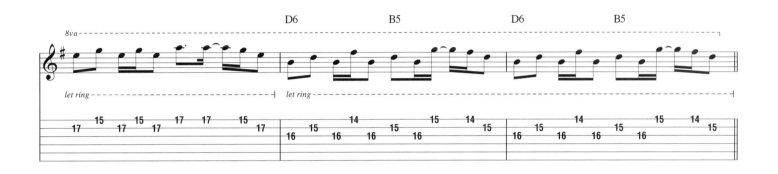

Chorus

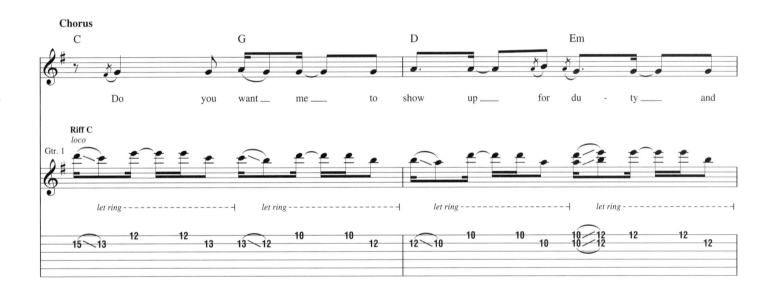

Do you want ___ me ___ to show up ___ for du - ty ___ and

Riff C

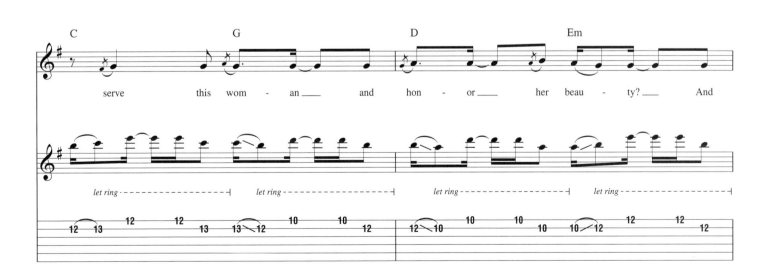

serve this wom - an ___ and hon - or ___ her beau - ty? ___ And

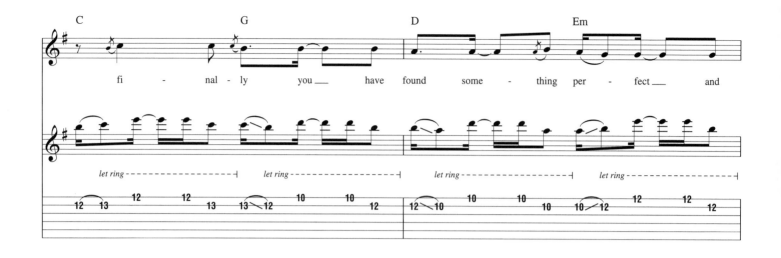

fi - nal - ly you ___ have found some - thing per - fect ___ and

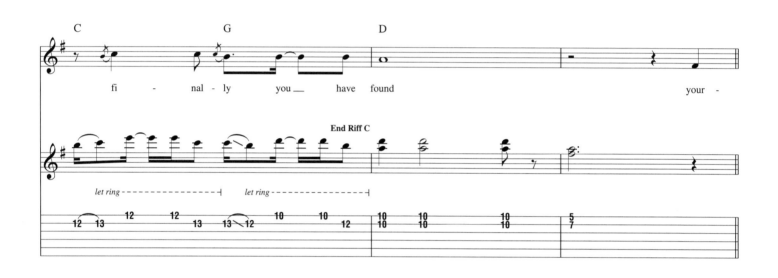

fi - nal - ly you ___ have found your -

End Riff C

Bridge

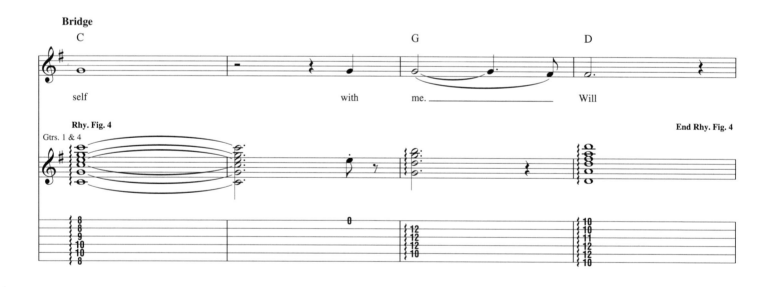

self with me. ___ Will

Rhy. Fig. 4

Gtrs. 1 & 4

End Rhy. Fig. 4

Gtrs. 1 & 4: w/ Rhy. Fig. 4 (2 3/4 times)

you ___ a - gree to take this

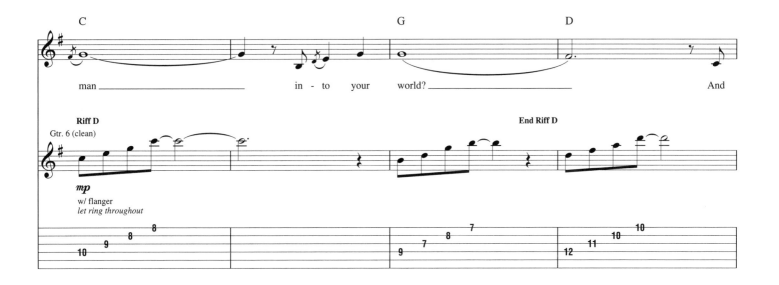

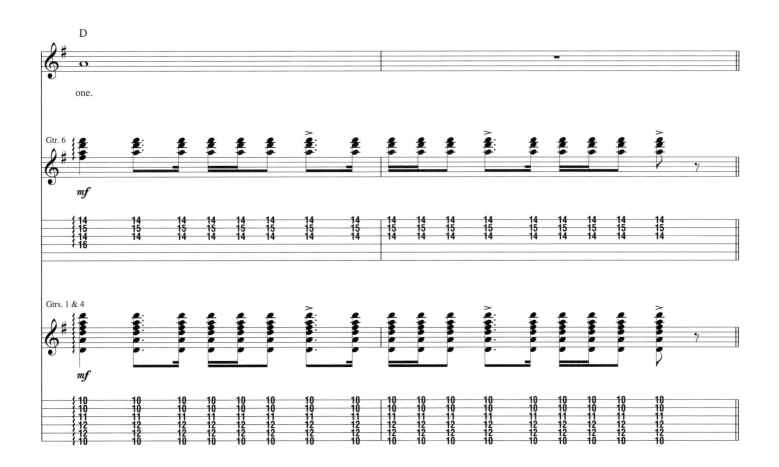

Verse

Gtr. 6 tacet

3. My lone rang - er, _____ the heat _____ ex - chang - er, _____ is

Gtr. 1 *8va*

let ring
*w/ octaver

Gtr. 4 **Riff E**

*w/ octaver

Gtr. 2

*w/ octaver

Gtr. 3

*w/ octaver

*Set for one octave above to simulate sped-up gtrs.

Chorus

Gtr. 1: w/ Riff C

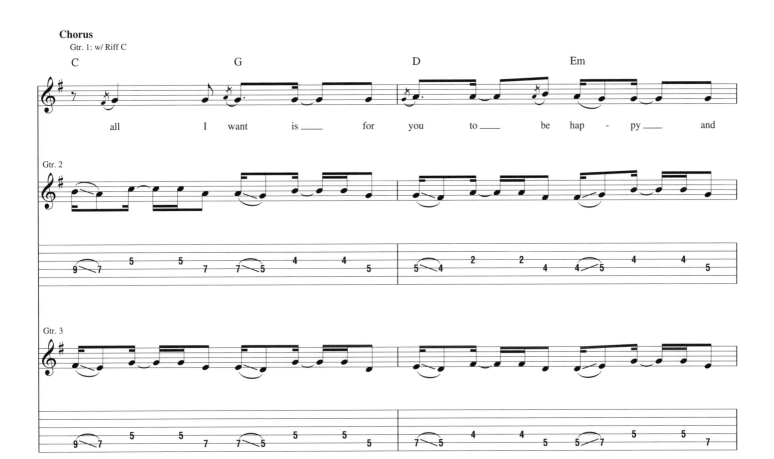

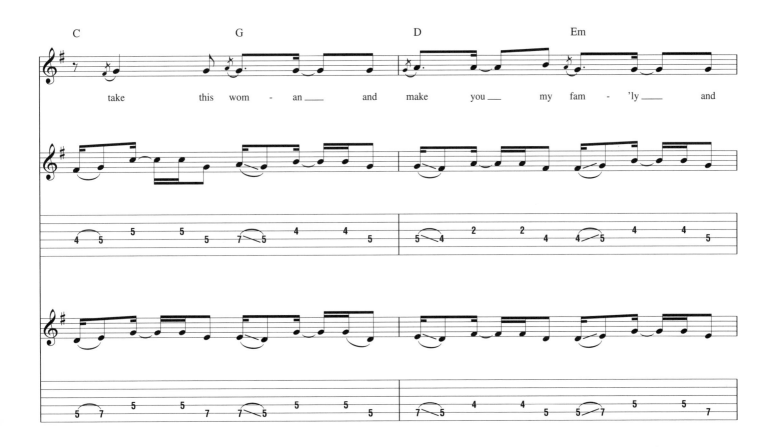

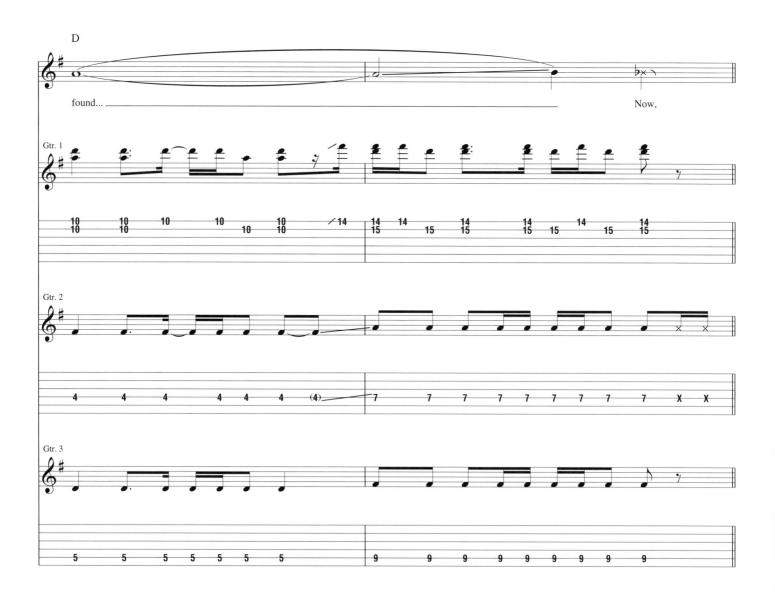

Outro-Chorus

all   I want   is ___   for   you   to ___   be   hap - py ___   and

Gtrs. 1, 2, 3, 7 & 8: w/ Riffs F, F1, F2, F3 & F4 (2 times)

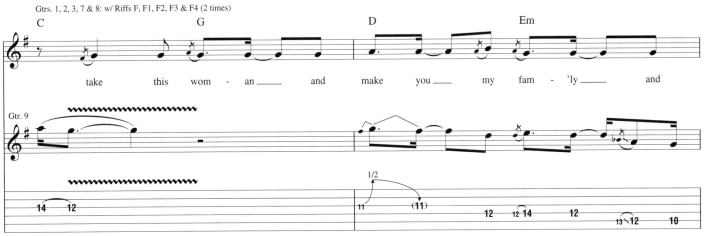

take   this   wom - an ___   and   make   you ___   my   fam - 'ly ___   and

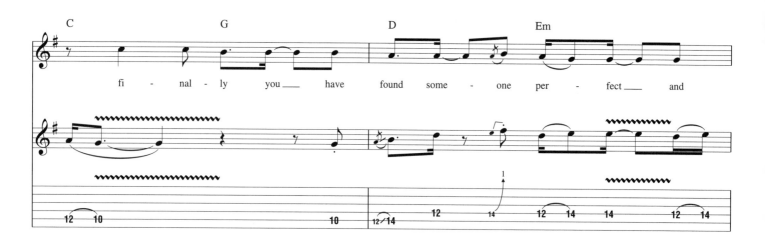

fi - nal - ly you___ have found some - one per - fect___ and

fi - nal - ly you___ have found _____ your - self.

21st Century

Words and Music by Anthony Kiedis, Flea, John Frusciante and Chad Smith

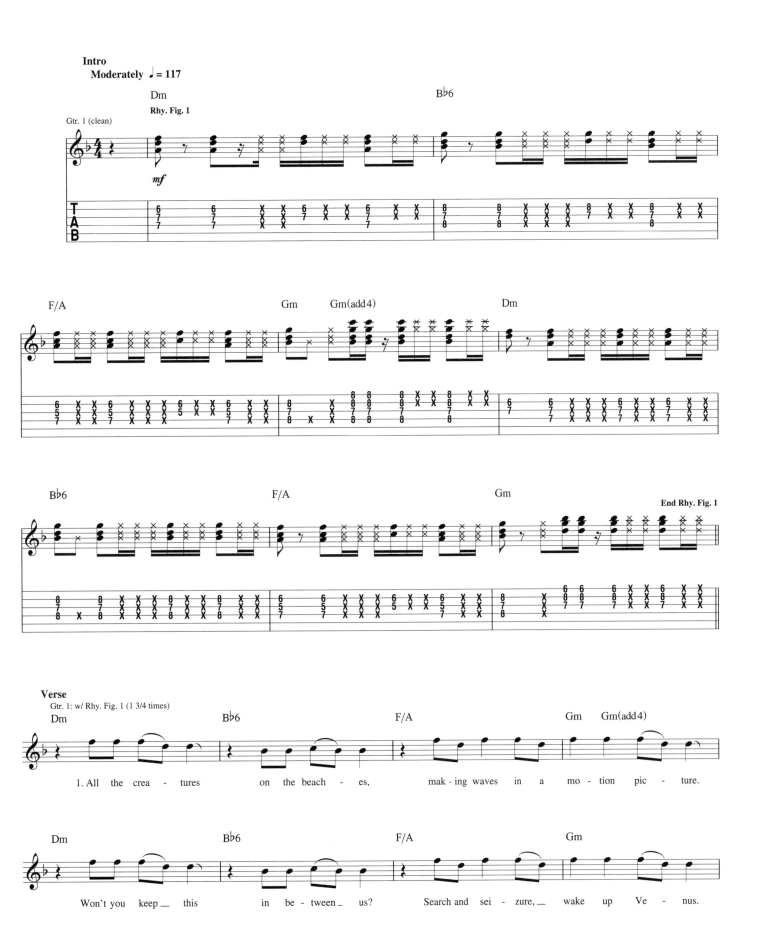

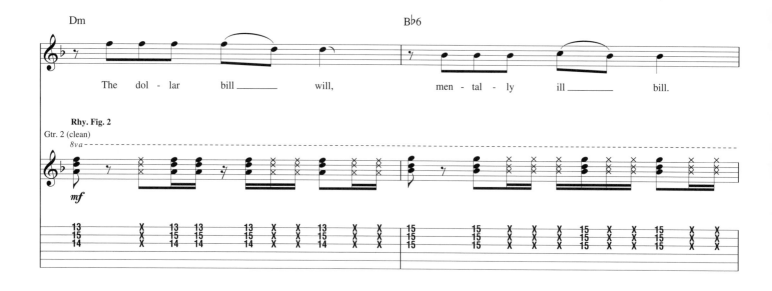

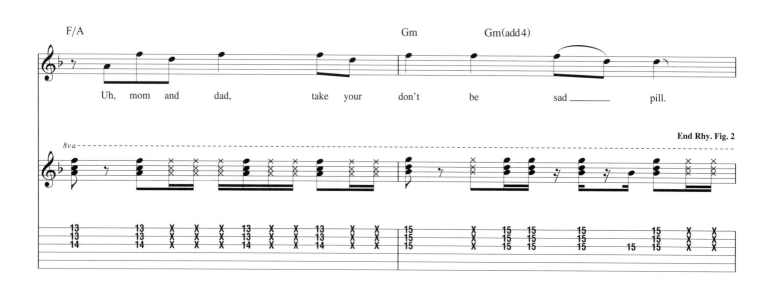

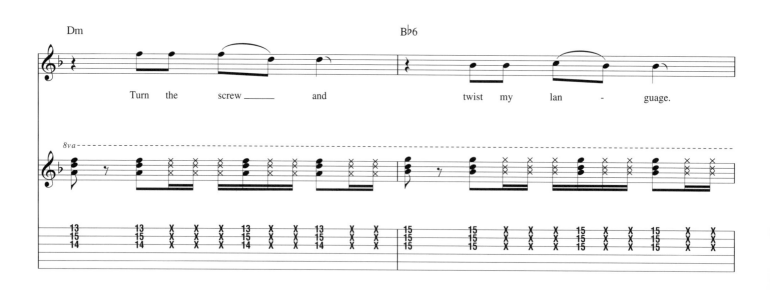

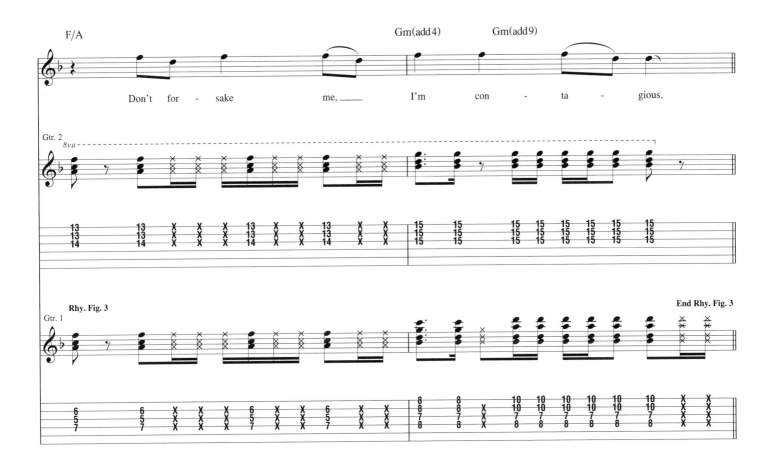

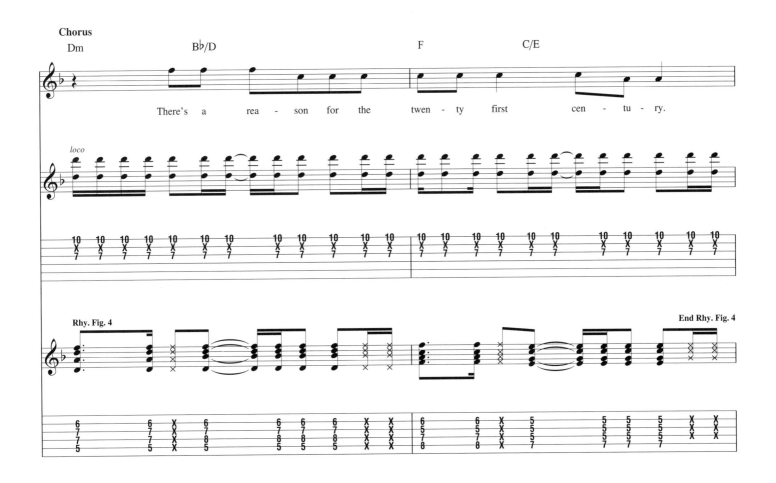

Not too sure,_____ but I know that it's meant to be_____

and that it's meant to be._____

Come on!

Woo!

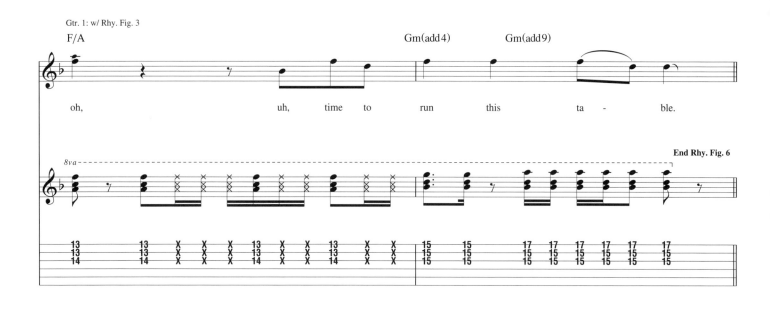

Chorus

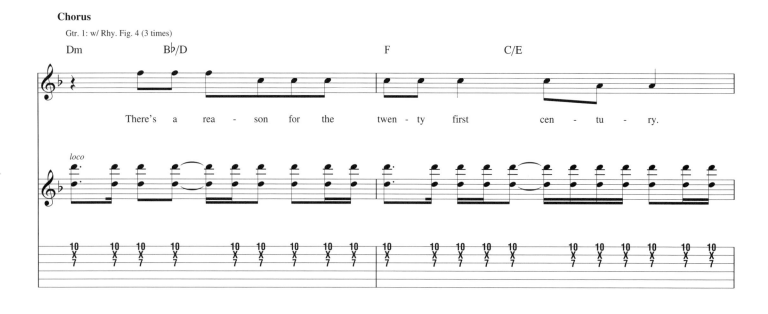

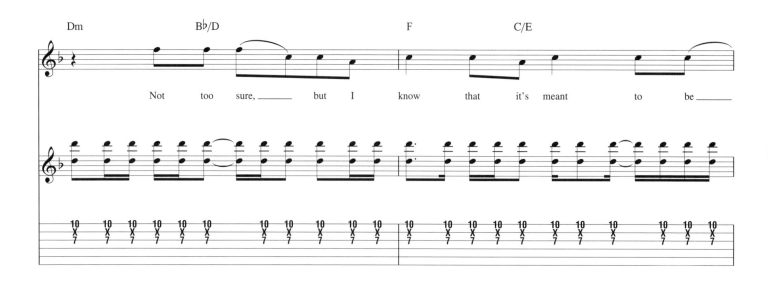

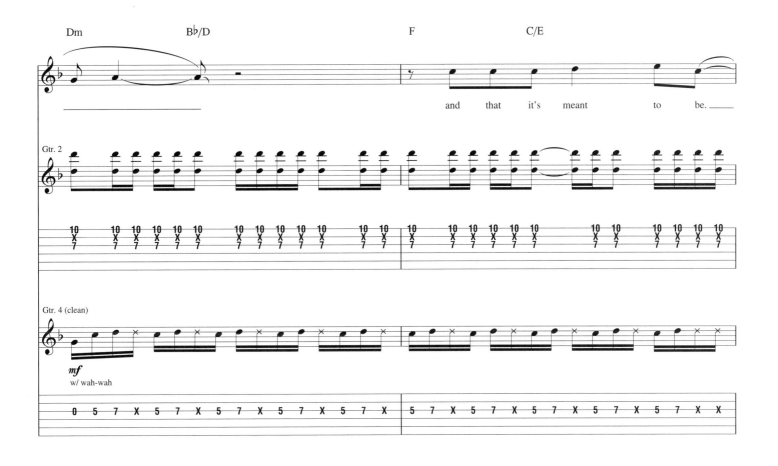

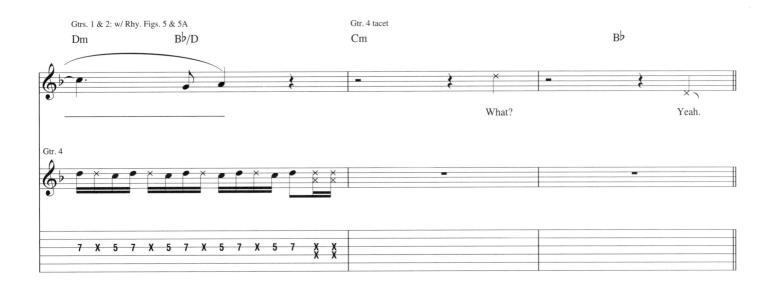

Interlude

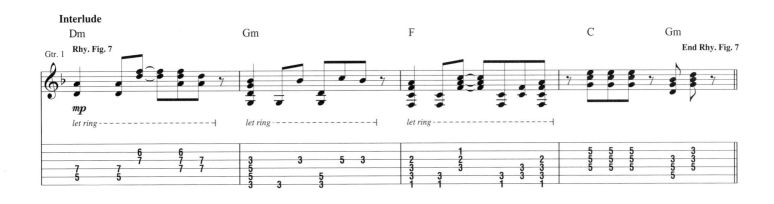

Bridge

Read me your scrip - ture and   read me your scrip - ture.   Read me your scrip - ture and

I   will   twist it.   Show me your wrist ___ and I,   show me your wrist ___ and

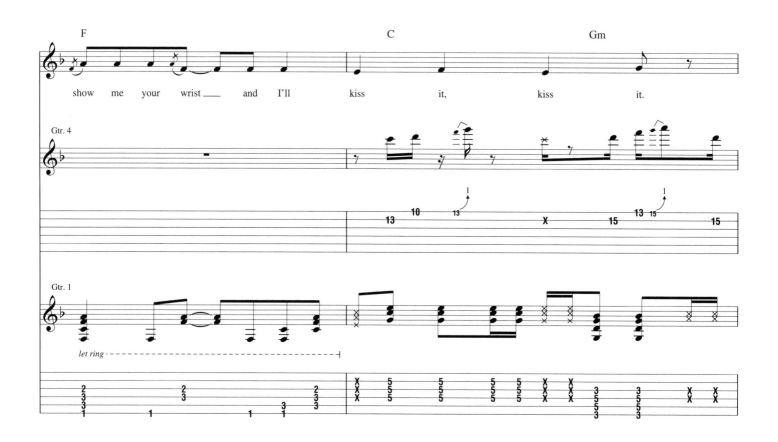

show me your wrist ___ and I'll   kiss   it,   kiss   it.

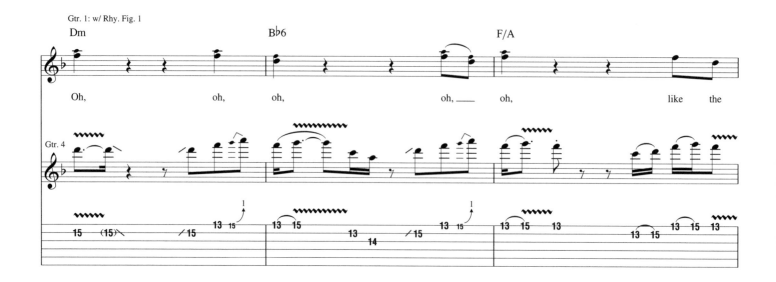

Oh,   oh,   oh,   oh, ___ oh,   like   the

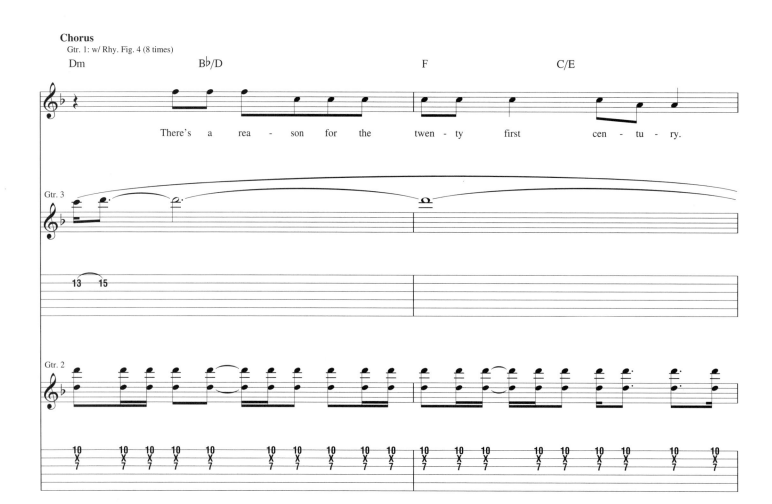

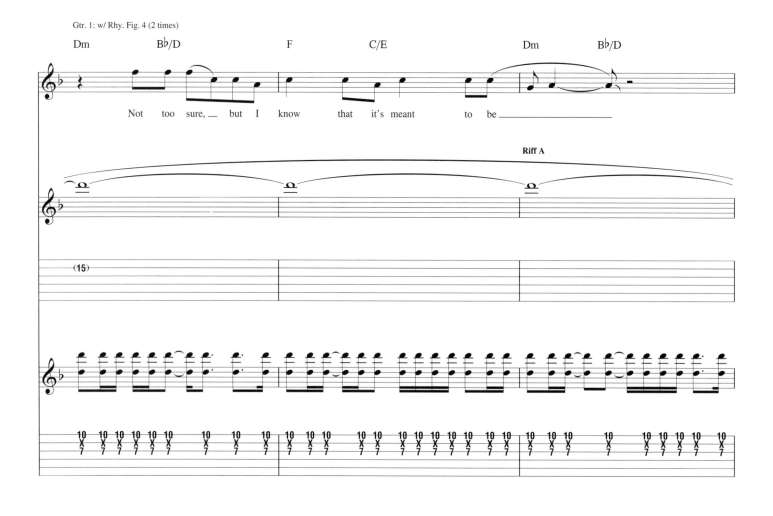

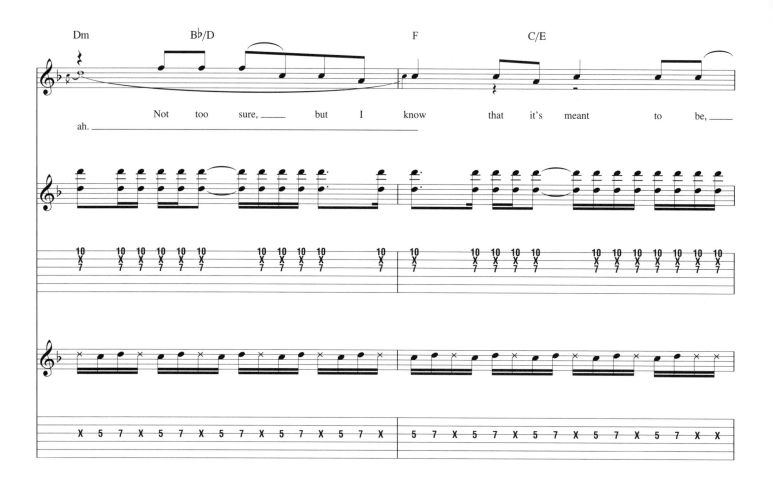

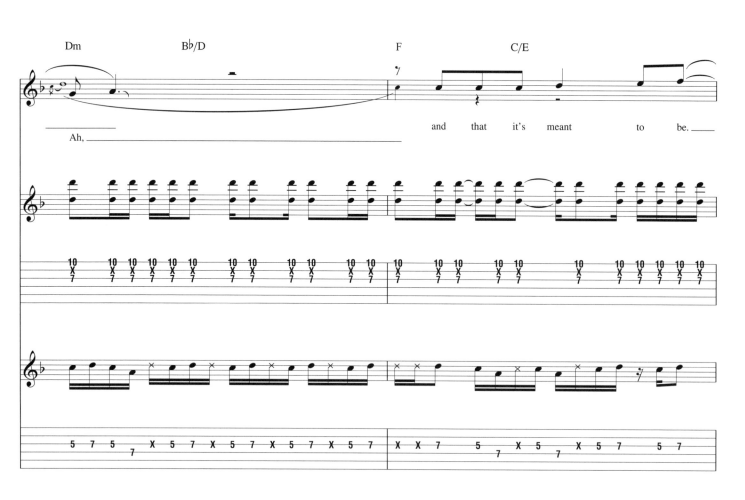

Outro-Guitar Solo

Gtr. 3: w/ Riff A (4 times)
Gtrs. 2 & 4 tacet

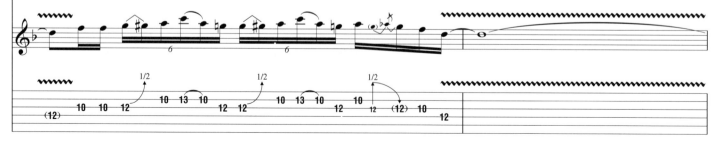

Pitch: D

*Microphinic fdbk., not caused by string vibration.

She Looks to Me

Words and Music by Anthony Kiedis, Flea, John Frusciante and Chad Smith

*Chord symbols reflect implied harmony.

dy-in' from the likes of a-ban - don-ment.   Lost in the val-ley with-out___ my hors - es.

She needs some-bod — y to hold.___

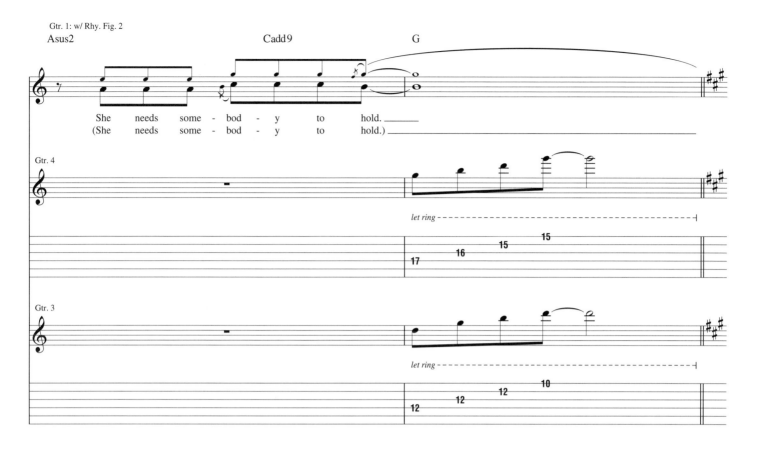

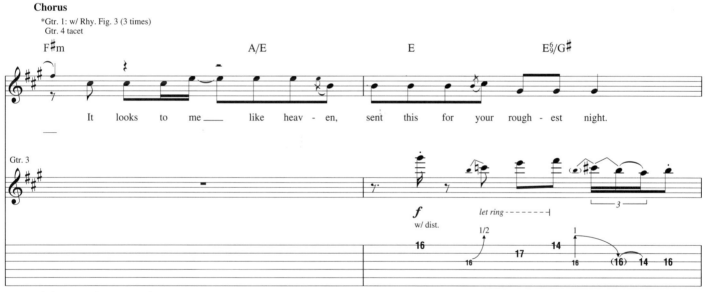

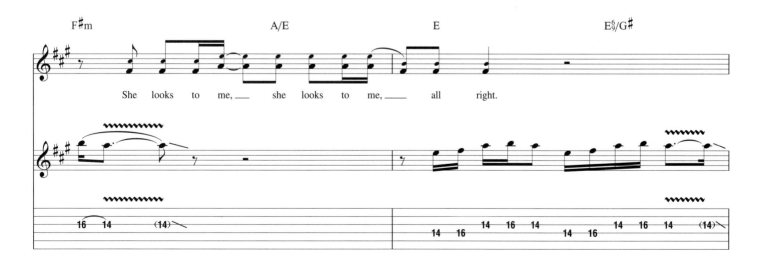

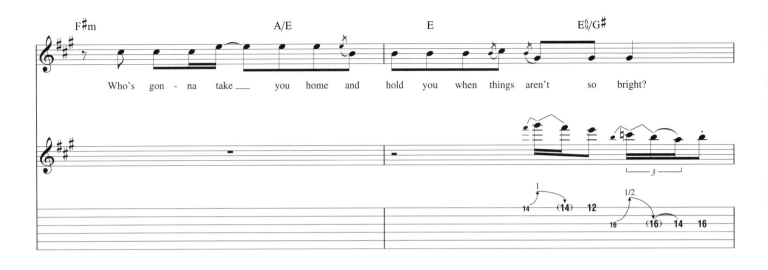

Who's gon - na take ___ you home and hold you when things aren't so bright?

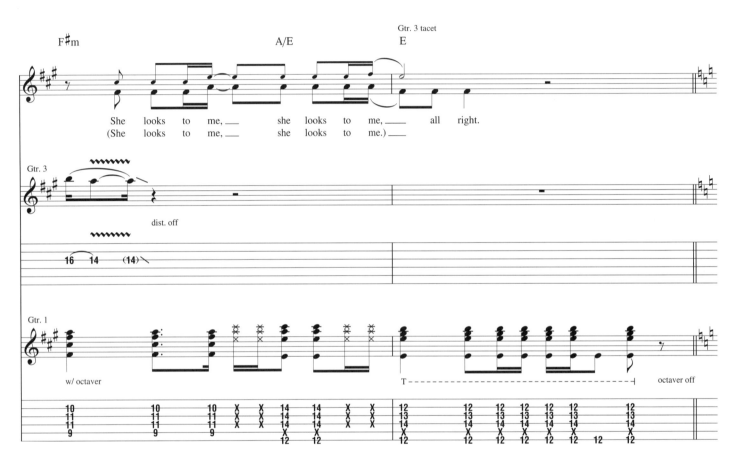

She looks to me, ___ she looks to me, ___ all right.
(She looks to me, ___ she looks to me.) ___

Bridge

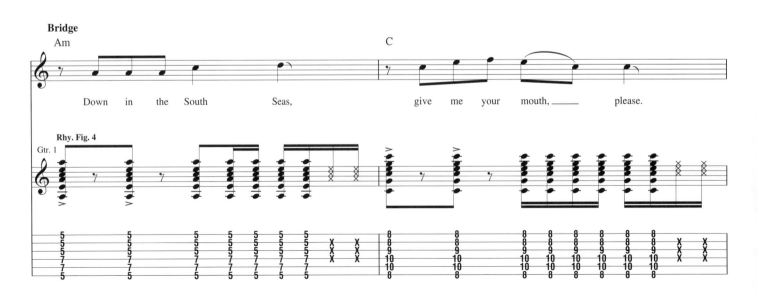

Down in the South Seas, give me your mouth, ___ please.

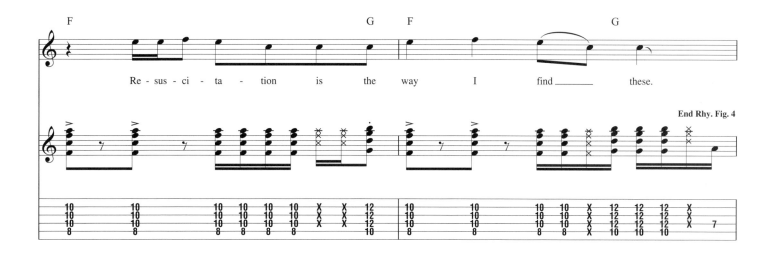

Re - sus - ci - ta - tion is the way I find _____ these.

End Rhy. Fig. 4

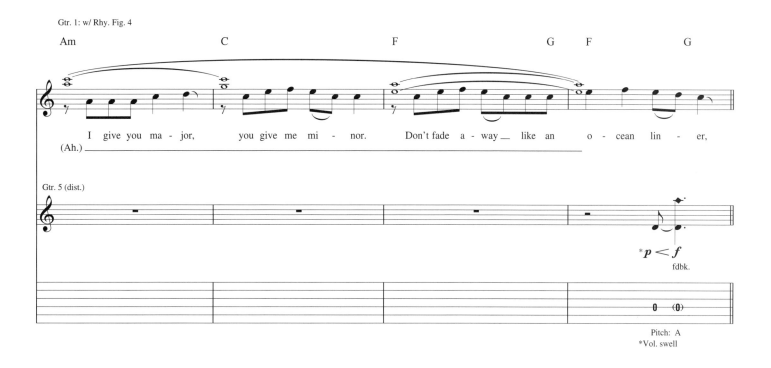

Gtr. 1: w/ Rhy. Fig. 4

I give you ma - jor, you give me mi - nor. Don't fade a - way _____ like an o - cean lin - er,
(Ah.) _____

Gtr. 5 (dist.)

$p < f$
fdbk.

Pitch: A
*Vol. swell

Guitar Solo

Gtr. 1: w/ Rhy. Fig. 1 (2 times)

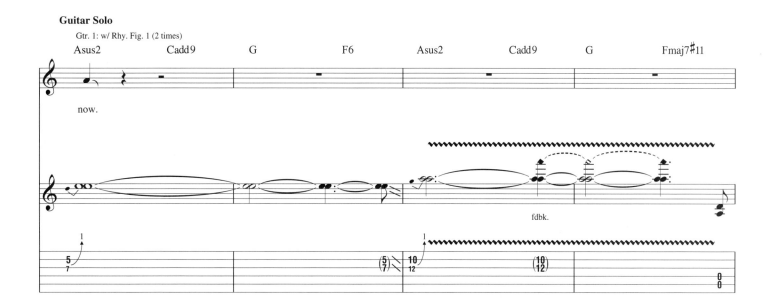

now.

fdbk.

Chorus

Gtr. 1: w/ Rhy. Fig. 3 (3 times)
Gtr. 4 tacet

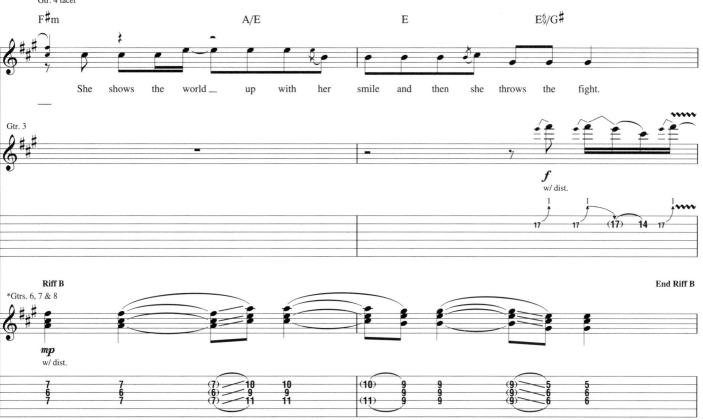

She shows the world __ up with her smile and then she throws the fight.

Gtr. 3

 f
w/ dist.

Riff B
*Gtrs. 6, 7 & 8

End Riff B

mp
w/ dist.

*Three gtrs., each playing single notes

Gtrs. 6, 7 & 8: w/ Riff B (2 times)

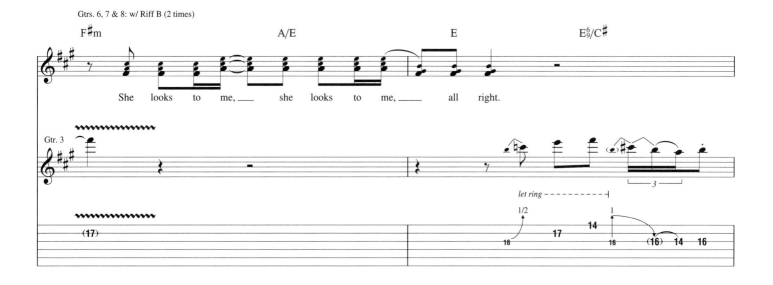

She looks to me, __ she looks to me, __ all right.

Gtr. 3

let ring

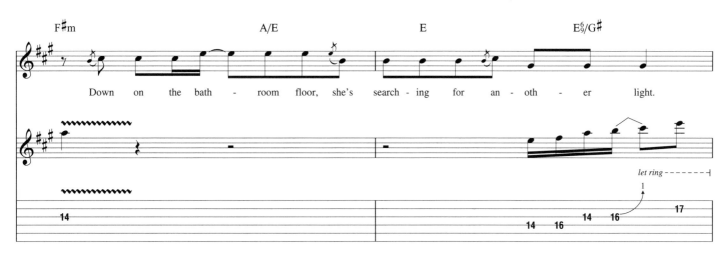

Down on the bath-room floor, she's search-ing for an-oth-er light.

let ring

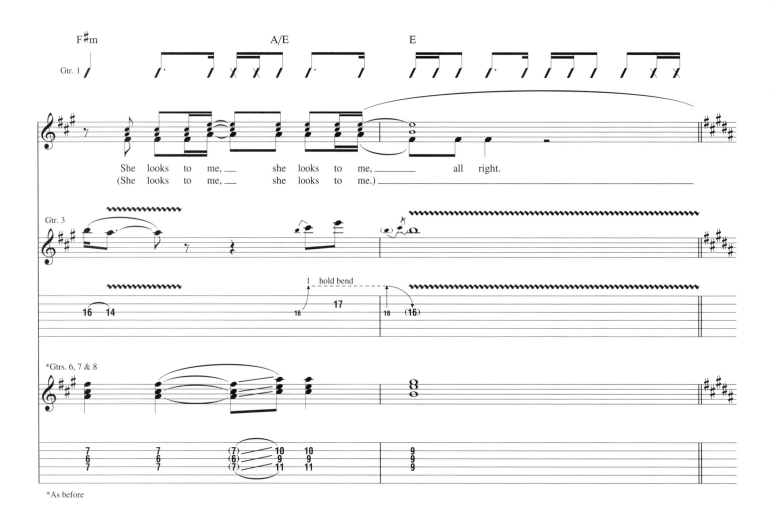

She looks to me, ___ she looks to me, ___ all right.
(She looks to me, ___ she looks to me.)

*As before

Chorus

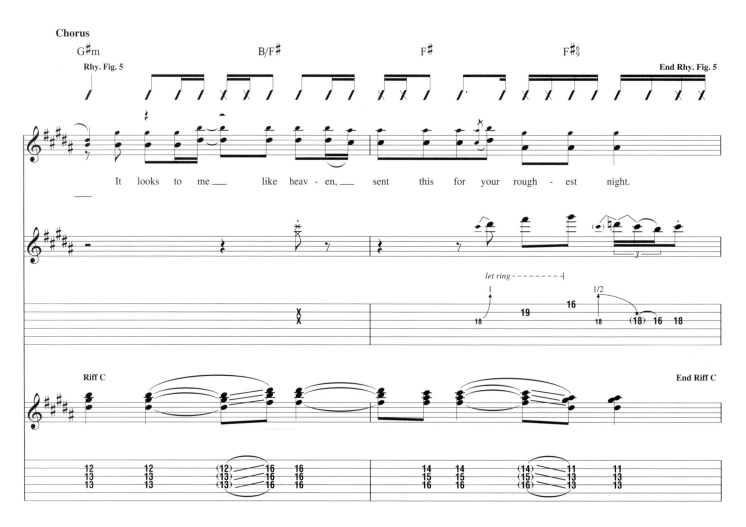

It looks to me ___ like heav-en, ___ sent this for your rough-est night.

Gtr. 1: w/ Rhy. Fig. 5 (3 times)
Gtrs. 6, 7 & 8: w/ Riff C (3 times)

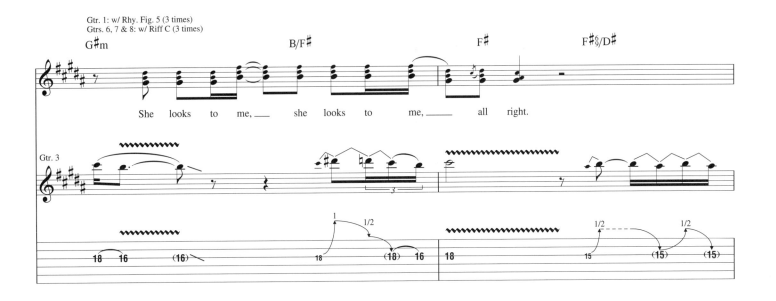

She looks to me, ____ she looks to me, ____ all right.

Who's gon-na take ____ you home and ____ hold you when things aren't ____ so bright?

She looks to me, ____ she looks to me.
(She looks to me, ____ she looks to me.) ____

199

Outro

Gtr. 1: w/ Rhy. Fig. 5 (3 times)
Gtrs. 6, 7 & 8: w/ Riff C (3 times)

Gtr. 3 tacet

Readymade

Words and Music by Anthony Kiedis, Flea, John Frusciante and Chad Smith

Intro
Moderately ♩ = 151

* Em7

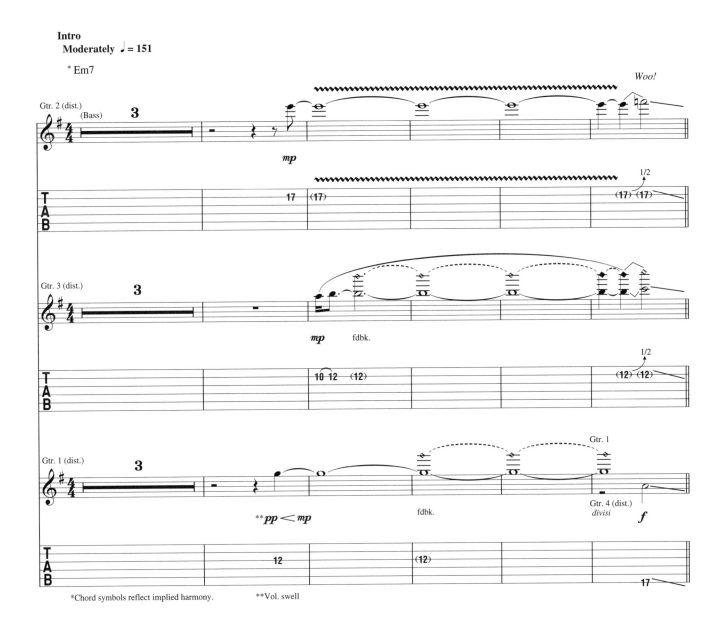

*Chord symbols reflect implied harmony.   **Vol. swell

Half-time feel
Gtrs. 1, 2 & 3 tacet

***Gtrs. 4 & 5

Riff A

End Riff A

***Gtr. 5 (dist.) played *f*.

Verse

Gtr. 4: w/ Riff A (5 times)
Gtr. 5: w/ Riff A (2 times)

1. Read - y - made, read - y - made, stead - y as the rhy - thm rolls. _____ Uh,

read - y - made, read - y - made, and this is how the stor - y goes. _____ I've got a

cous - in mak - in' beats deep down in Ar - i - zo - na. _____ We're gon - na

rock - et to Ra - mone's in the cit - y of Po - mo - na. _____ Oh,

read - y - made, read - y - made, stead - y as the rhy - thm rolls. _____

Read - y - made, read - y - made, and this is how the stor - y goes. _____

Chorus

Verse

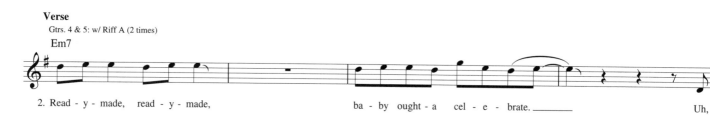

2. Read - y - made, read - y - made, ba - by ought - a cel - e - brate. _____ Uh,

read - y - made, read - y - made, and now it's time to de - vi - ate. _____ I've got a

sis - ter mak - in' ba - bies with a Black and Deck - er blow torch. _____ We gon - na

bop it all night in the mid - dle of the back porch. _____ Yeah,

read - y - made, read - y - made, ba - by ought - a cel - e - brate. _____ Uh,

read-y-made,   read-y-made,   and now it's time to de-vi-ate. _____

Gtrs. 4 & 5

Chorus

Bkgd. Voc.: w/ Voc. Fig. 1
*Gtrs. 4 & 5: w/ Rhy. Fig. 1

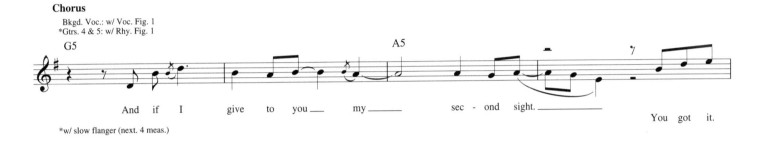

G5   A5

And   if   I   give   to   you ___   my _____   sec - ond   sight. _____

You   got   it.

*w/ slow flanger (next. 4 meas.)

Gtrs. 4 & 5: w/ Riff C

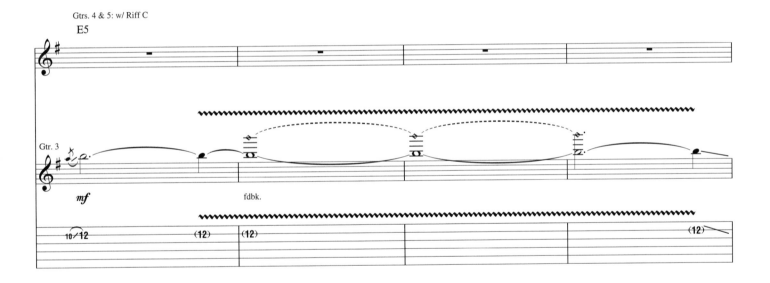

E5

Gtr. 3

mf   fdbk.

Gtr. 3 tacet
**Gtrs. 4 & 5: w/ Rhy. Fig. 1

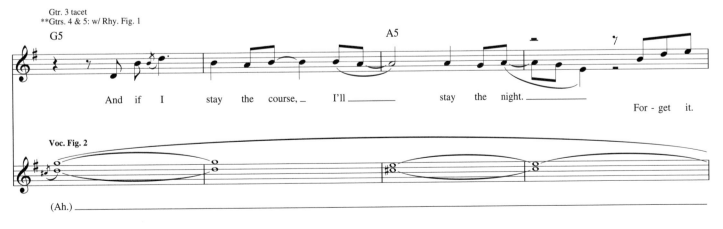

G5   A5

And   if   I   stay   the   course, _   I'll _____   stay   the   night. _____

For - get   it.

Voc. Fig. 2

(Ah.) _____

**w/ slow flanger (next 4 meas.)

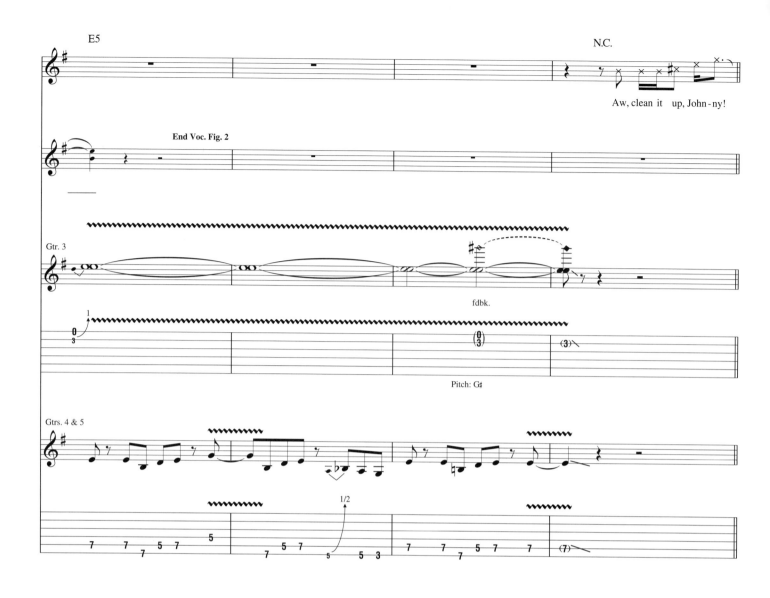

Aw, clean it   up, John-ny!

Guitar Solo

Gtr. 3 tacet
Gtr. 5: w/ Riff A (4 times)

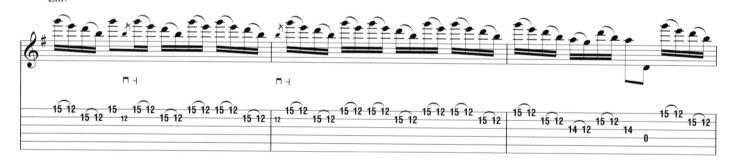

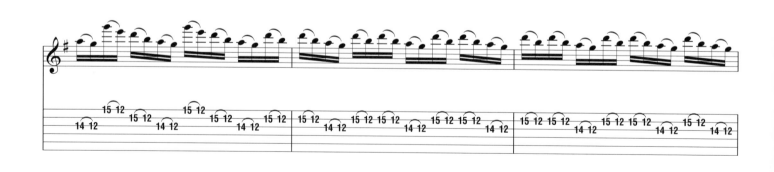

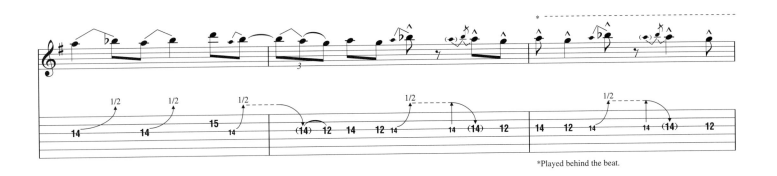

*Played behind the beat.

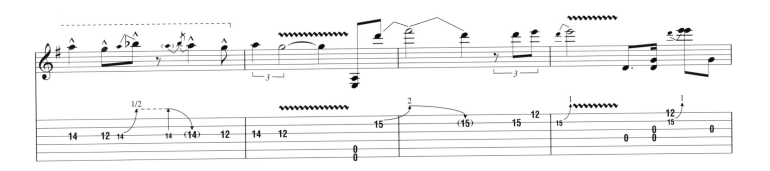

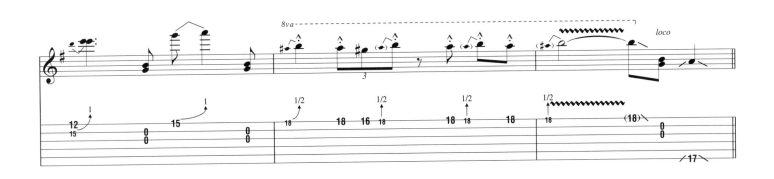

Interlude

w/ Voc. ad lib. (next 3 meas.)

D5   D5/C#   B5   N.C.

Gtrs. 4 & 5

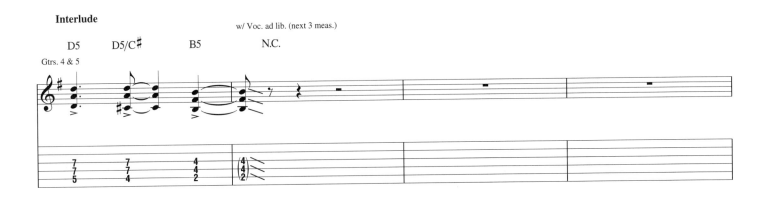

w/ Voc. ad lib. (next 3 meas.)

A5   E/G#   F#5   N.C.   D5   D5/C#   B5

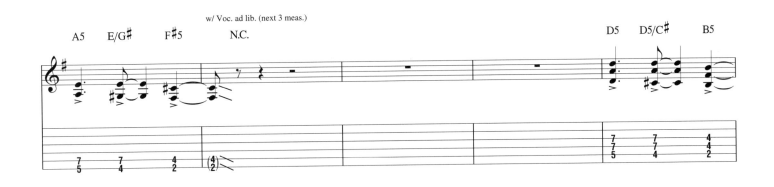

w/ Voc. ad lib. (next 3 meas.)

N.C.   A5   E/G#   F#5

N.C.

grad. bend

Verse
Gtrs. 4 & 5: w/ Riff A (2 times)

Em7

3. Read - y - made, read - y - made,   uh, rock - in' for the sake of slade. _____   Uh,

read - y - made, read - y - made, ____   uh, lis - ten but don't be a - fraid. ____   I got a

*Gtrs. 4 & 5: w/ Riff D

broth - er mak - in' trou - ble in the state of Cal - e - do - nia. _____   I wish I

*w/ octaver set for one octave above (next 8 meas.).

knew an - oth - er way, but I'm gon - na have to clone ya. _____   Hell!

Gtr. 3: w/ Riff B (1 1/2 times)
Gtrs. 4 & 5: w/ Riff A (1 1/2 times)

E7

Read - y - made, read - y - made,   uh, rock - in' for the sake of slade. _____

_____   Uh, read - y - made, read - y - made,   uh,

lis - ten but don't be a - fraid.

Chorus

And if I give to you ___ my ___ sec - ond sight... ___

You got it.

If

Words and Music by Anthony Kiedis, Flea, John Frusciante and Chad Smith

*Chord symbols reflect overall harmony.

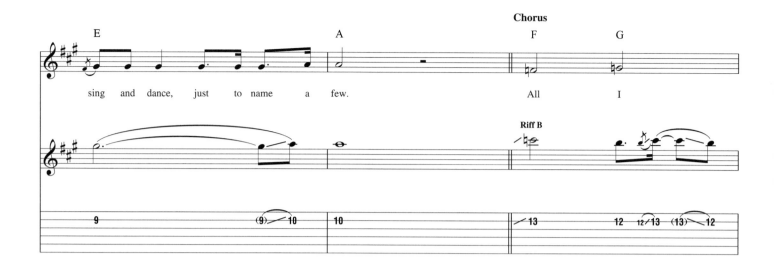

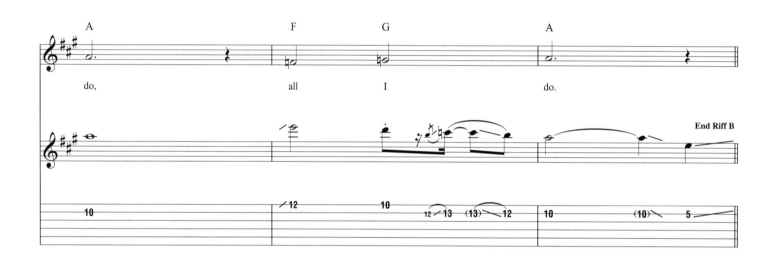

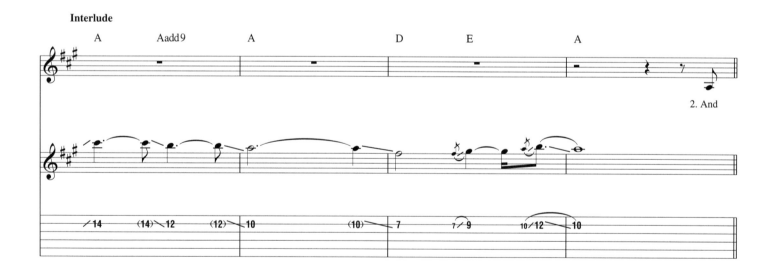

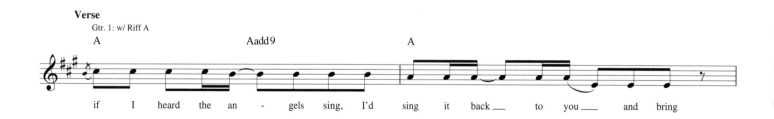

sound of heav - en ring - ing just for you. And

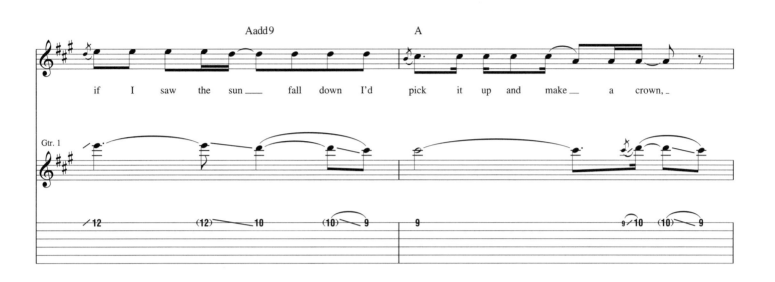

if I saw the sun ___ fall down I'd pick it up and make ___ a crown, ___

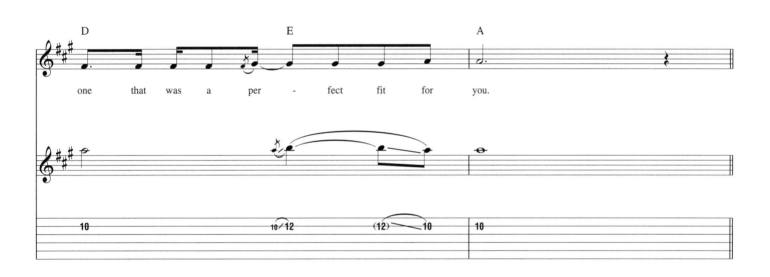

one that was a per - fect fit for you.

Pre-Chorus

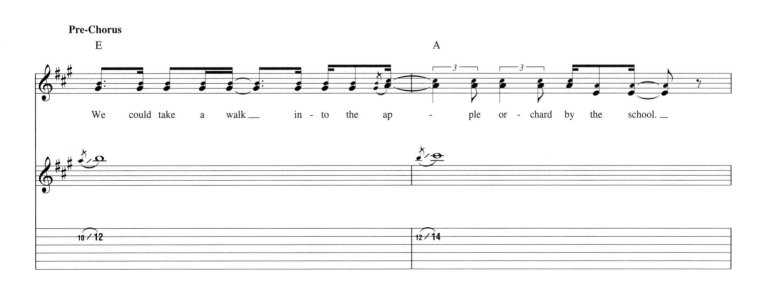

We could take a walk ___ in - to the ap - ple or - chard by the school. ___

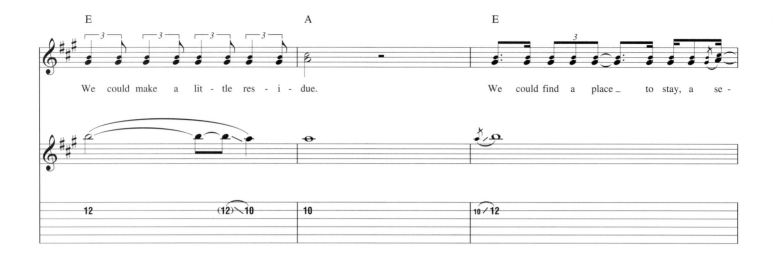

We could make a lit - tle res - i - due. We could find a place _ to stay, a se -

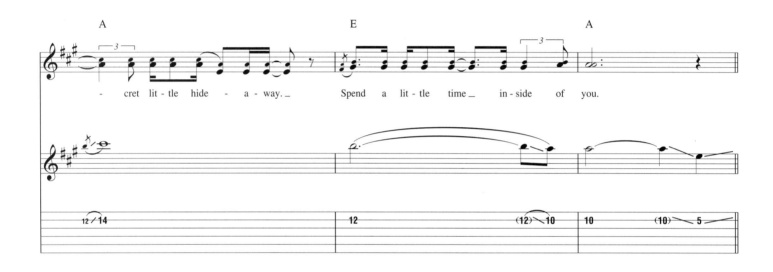

- cret lit - tle hide - a - way. _ Spend a lit - tle time _ in - side of you.

Chorus
Gtr. 1: w/ Riff B

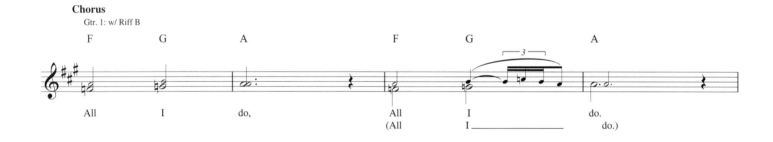

All I do, All I do.
(All I _____ do.)

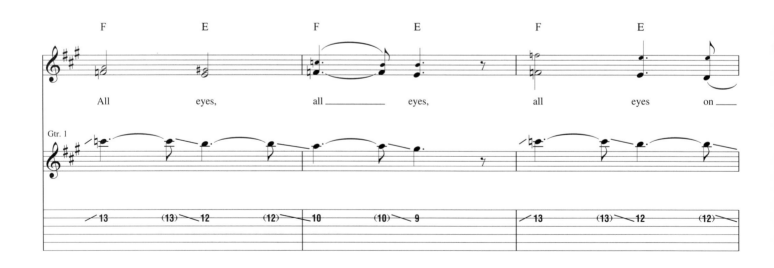

All eyes, all _____ eyes, all eyes on _____

Gtr. 1

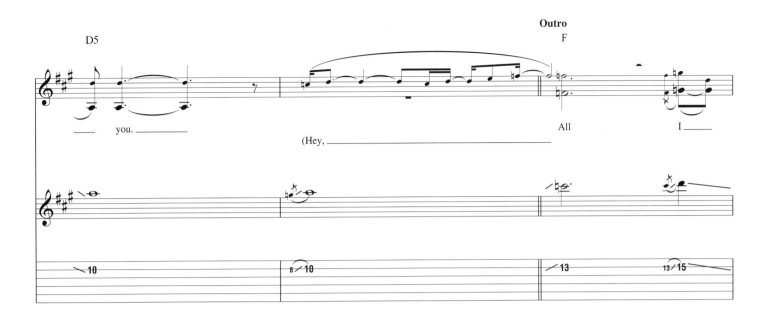

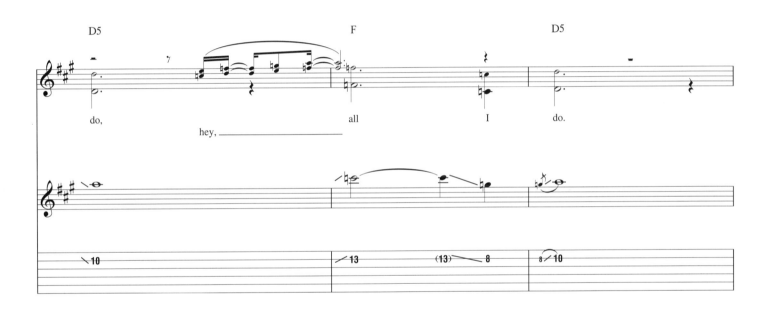

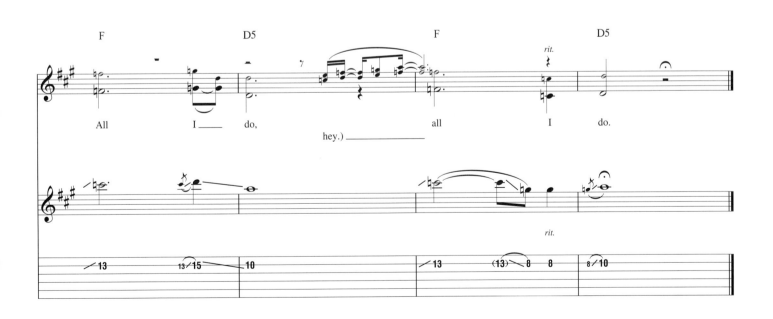

Make You Feel Better

Words and Music by Anthony Kiedis, Flea, John Frusciante and Chad Smith

Interlude

Oh yeah!

Verse

3. In the world that has run a - mok, __ I got to set my sights just to get struck. __ I,
(Ah.) _____

I walk a - way from the rank and file, __ uh, with a punched out mouth and a pack of style. __ I said,
(Ah.) _____

She's the one, she's the on - ly one __ to make me search my - self un - til I'm done __ and
(Ah.) _____

tell me now in a tel - e - gram, __ uh, do the sea of stars make a dia - a - gram? __ And
(Ah.) _____

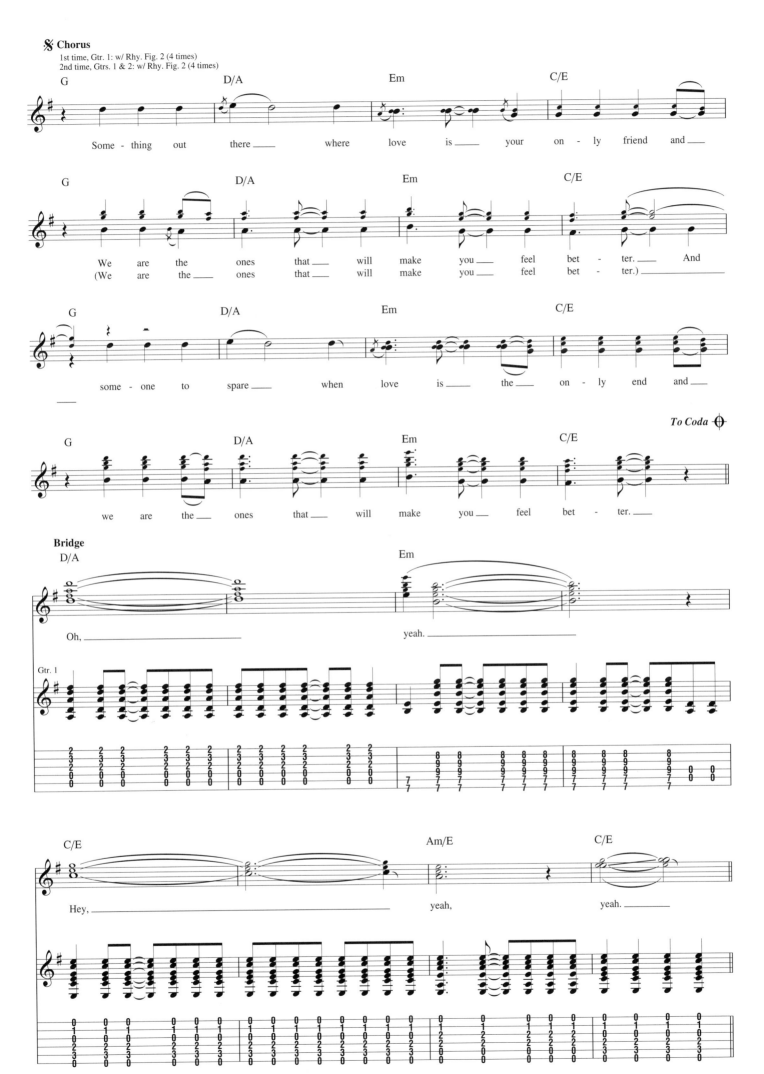

Chorus

1st time, Gtr. 1: w/ Rhy. Fig. 2 (4 times)
2nd time, Gtrs. 1 & 2: w/ Rhy. Fig. 2 (4 times)

G   D/A   Em   C/E

Some - thing out there ____ where love is ____ your on - ly friend and ____

G   D/A   Em   C/E

We are the ones that ____ will make you ____ feel bet - ter. ____ And
(We are the ____ ones that ____ will make you ____ feel bet - ter.)

G   D/A   Em   C/E

some - one to spare ____ when love is ____ the ____ on - ly end and ____

To Coda ⊕

G   D/A   Em   C/E

we are the ____ ones that ____ will make you ____ feel bet - ter. ____

Bridge

D/A   Em

Oh, _____   yeah.

Gtr. 1

C/E   Am/E   C/E

Hey, _____ yeah,   yeah. ____

219

Interlude

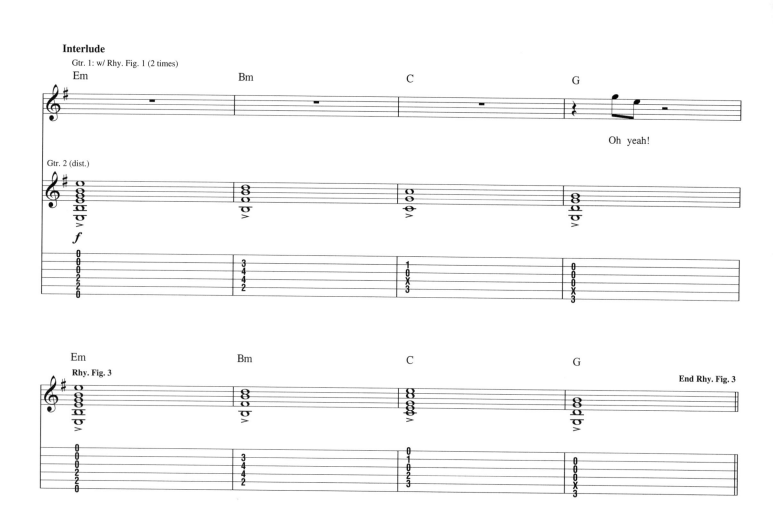

Oh yeah!

Verse

4. So a - live, I ar - rive on dust. You could search my mind for the red on rust.__ I said

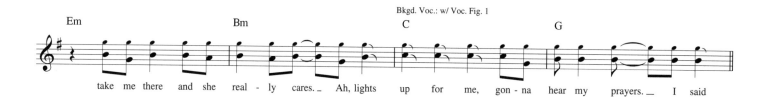

take me there and she real - ly cares.__ Ah, lights up for me, gon - na hear my prayers.__ I said

Pre-Chorus

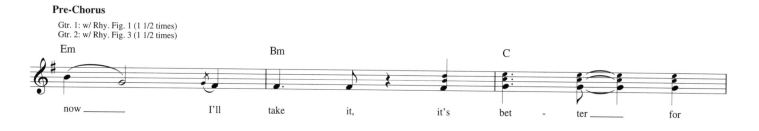

now _____ I'll take it, it's bet - ter _____ for

you. Some - how _____ we'll make it 'cause

220

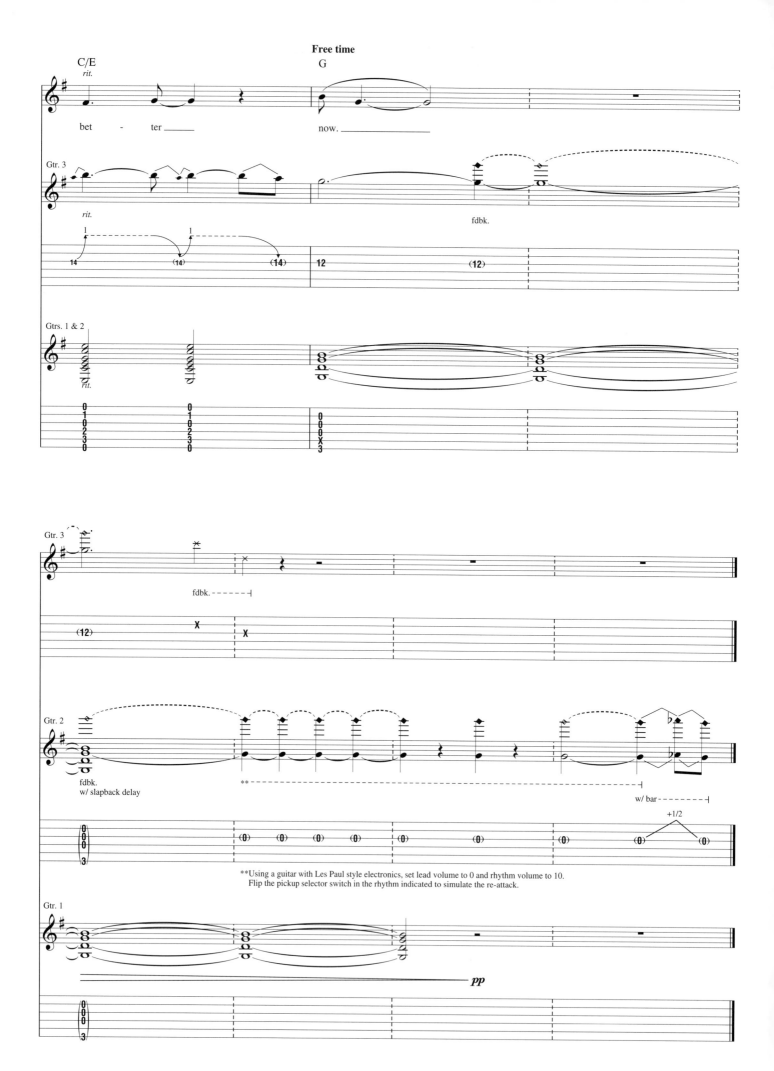

Free time

bet - ter _____ now. _____

fdbk. - - - - - - -|

**Using a guitar with Les Paul style electronics, set lead volume to 0 and rhythm volume to 10.
Flip the pickup selector switch in the rhythm indicated to simulate the re-attack.

pp

Animal Bar

Words and Music by Anthony Kiedis, Flea, John Frusciante and Chad Smith

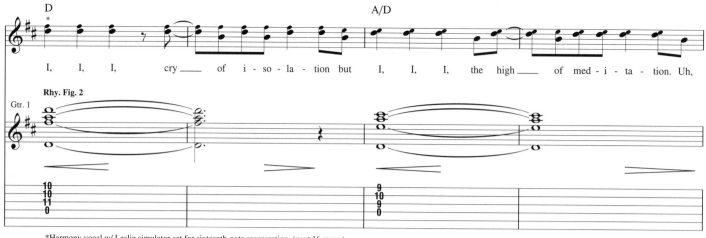

*Harmony vocal w/ Leslie simulator set for sixteenth-note regeneration. (next 16 meas.)

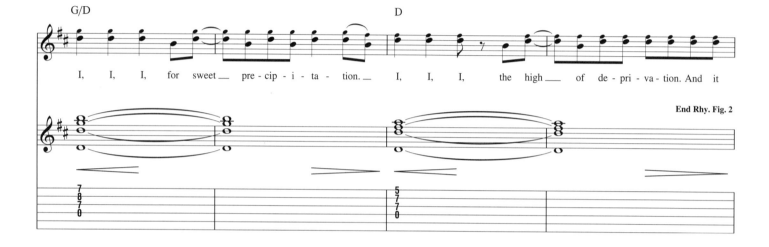

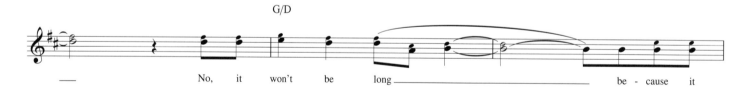

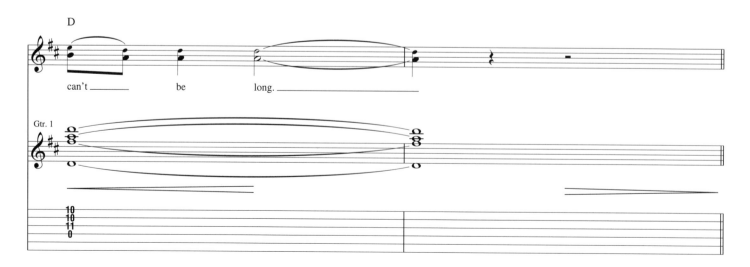

% Chorus

2nd time, Gtr. 2 tacet
3rd time, Gtrs. 5 & 6 tacet

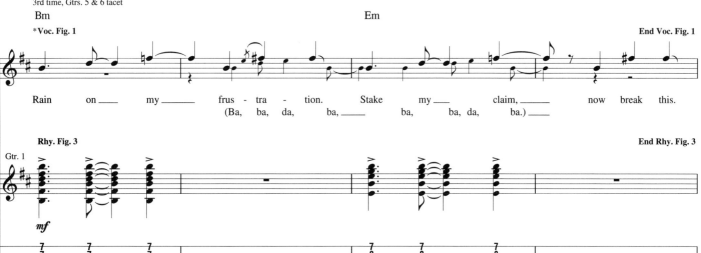

Rain on my frus-tra-tion. Stake my claim, now break this.
(Ba, ba, da, ba, ba, ba, da, ba.)

*Applies to downstemmed part.

Bkgd. Voc.: w/ Voc. Fig. 1
Gtr. 1: w/ Rhy. Fig. 3

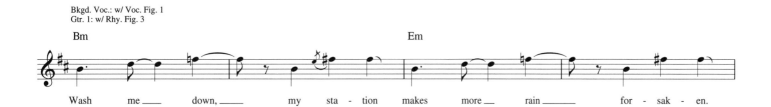

Wash me down, my sta-tion makes more rain for-sak-en.

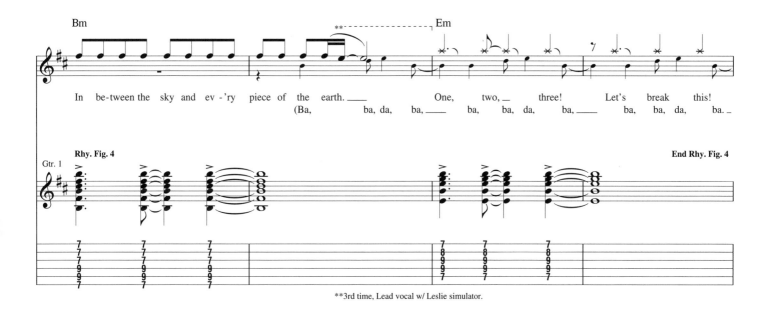

In be-tween the sky and ev-'ry piece of the earth. One, two, three! Let's break this!
(Ba, ba, da, ba, ba, ba, da, ba, ba, ba, da, ba.

**3rd time, Lead vocal w/ Leslie simulator.

To Coda 1 ⊕   *To Coda 2* ⊕

Gtr. 1: w/ Rhy. Fig. 4

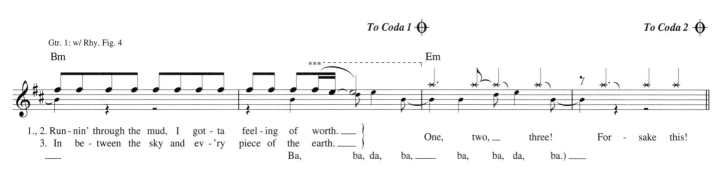

1., 2. Run-nin' through the mud, I got-ta feel-ing of worth.
3. In be-tween the sky and ev-'ry piece of the earth.
Ba, ba, da, ba, ba, ba, da, ba.)
One, two, three! For-sake this!

***3rd time, as before.

*Harmony vocals w/ Leslie simulator as before. (next 16 meas.)

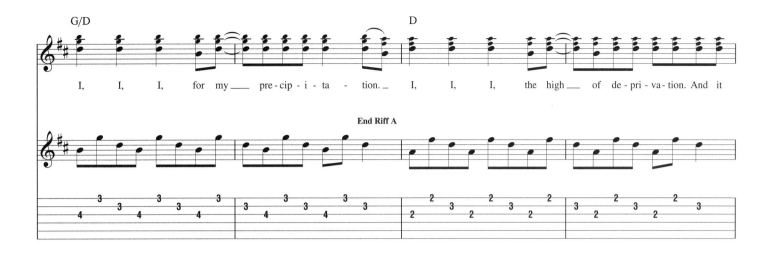

I, I, I, for my precip-i-ta-tion. I, I, I, the high of de-pri-va-tion. And it

won't be long. No, it won't be long.

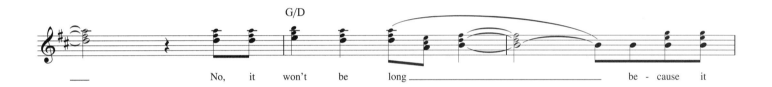

No, it won't be long be-cause it

D.S. al Coda 1

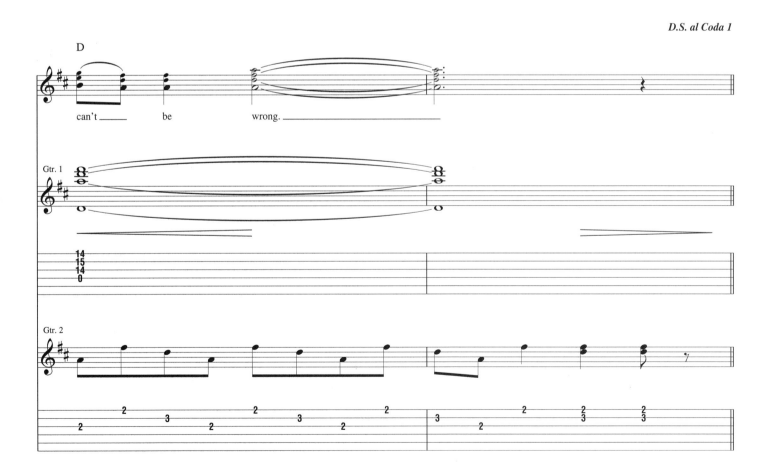

can't be wrong.

Coda 1

Guitar Solo

Gtr. 1: w/ Rhy. Fig. 1 (1st 2 meas.)

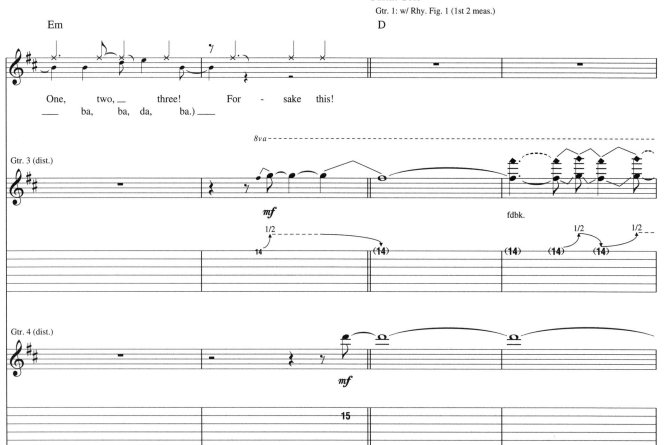

One, two, three! For - sake this!
ba, ba, da, ba.)

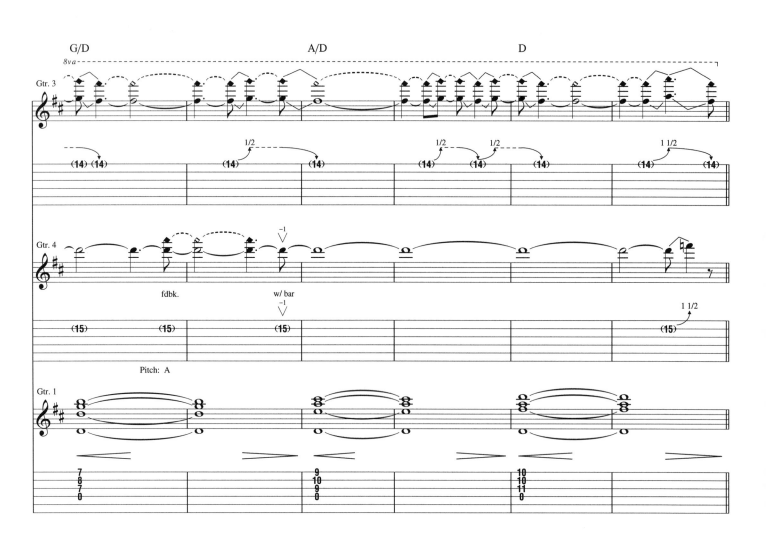

Bridge

Gtrs. 3 & 4 tacet

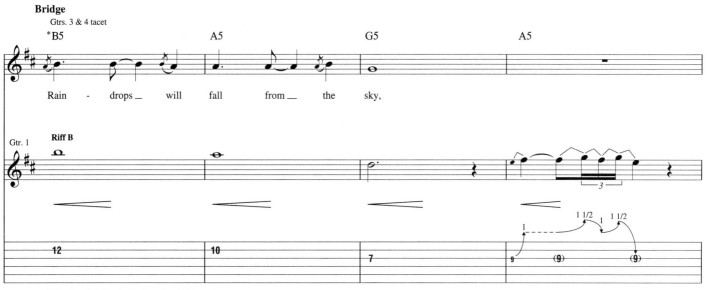

Rain - drops _ will fall from _ the sky,

Gtr. 1   **Riff B**

*Chord symbols implied by bass. (next 32 meas.)

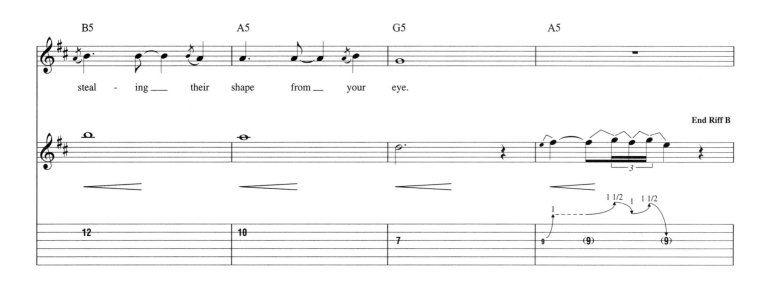

steal - ing __ their shape from __ your eye.

End Riff B

Now we __ can all get __ some sleep. __ The

Riff C   **End Riff C**

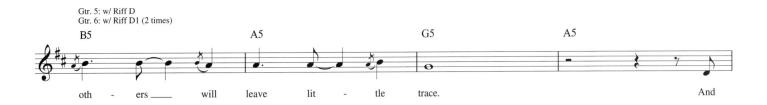

Gtr. 5: w/ Riff D
Gtr. 6: w/ Riff D1 (2 times)

oth - ers ___ will leave lit - tle trace. And

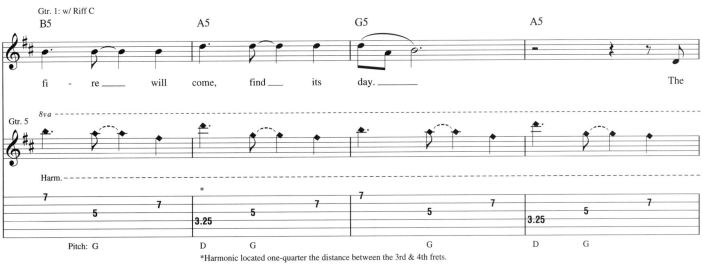

Gtr. 1: w/ Riff C

fi - re ___ will come, find ___ its day. ___ The

*Harmonic located one-quarter the distance between the 3rd & 4th frets.

D.S. al Coda 2

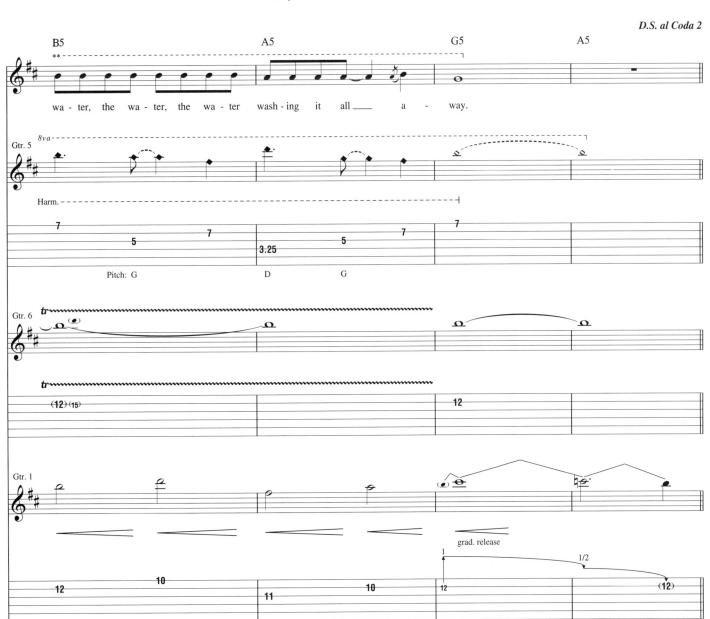

wa - ter, the wa - ter, the wa - ter wash - ing it all ___ a - way.

grad. release

**w/ Leslie simulator as before.

231

Coda 2

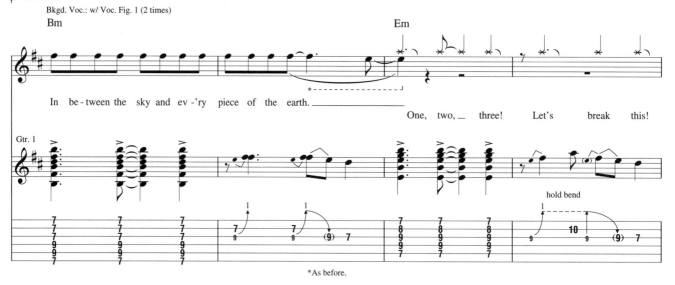

In be-tween the sky and ev-'ry piece of the earth.

One, two, — three! Let's break this!

*As before.

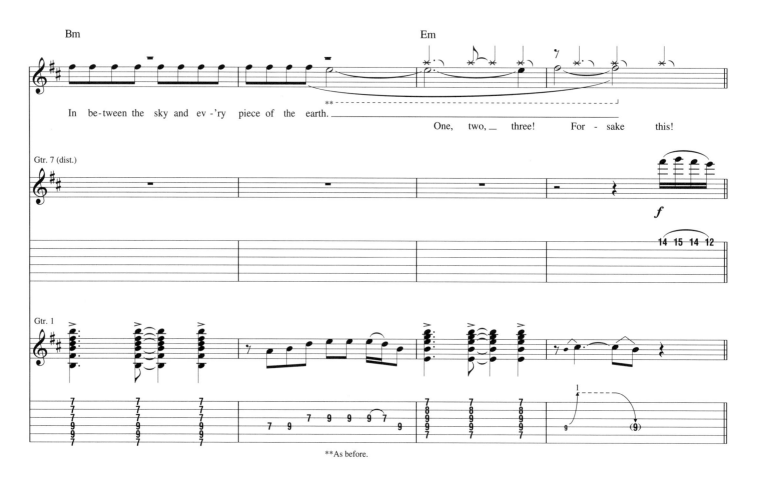

In be-tween the sky and ev -'ry piece of the earth.

One, two, — three! For - sake this!

**As before.

Outro-Guitar Solo
Half-time feel

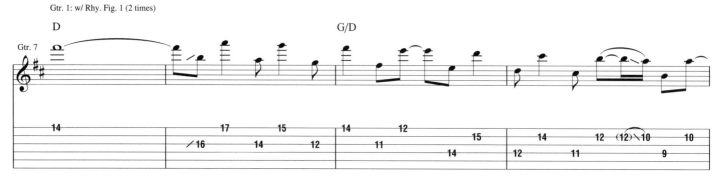

So Much I

Words and Music by Anthony Kiedis, Flea, John Frusciante and Chad Smith

Gtr. 1: w/ Riff C (1st 4 meas.)

F#m   A5/E   D5   A

Uh, so much _ I,   uh, wish I ____ could,   uh, so man - y I   wish I ____ would.

F#m   A5/E   Bm9

Uh, so much _ I   wish I ____ could   count on you not to de - feat me.

Gtr. 1   Riff D

End Riff D

let ring

%Chorus

A5   E5   B5

Please don't turn a - way ____ a - gain.

Rhy. Fig. 1

End Rhy. Fig. 1

w/ dist.

Gtr. 1: w/ Rhy. Fig. 1 (3 times)

A5   E5   B5

Please don't turn me ____ in - to them. ____

A5   E5   B5

Please don't turn a - way ____ a friend. ____

To Coda

A5   E5   B5

Please don't turn me ____ in - to them. ____ Ti, ti, tee.

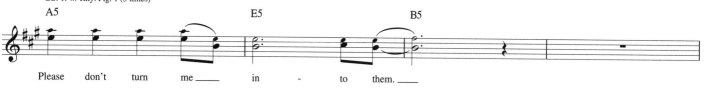

Interlude

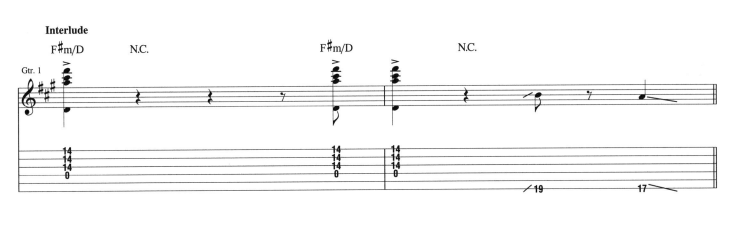

Verse

3. Stand _ by for the great e - clipse. _ Rip it out, now,

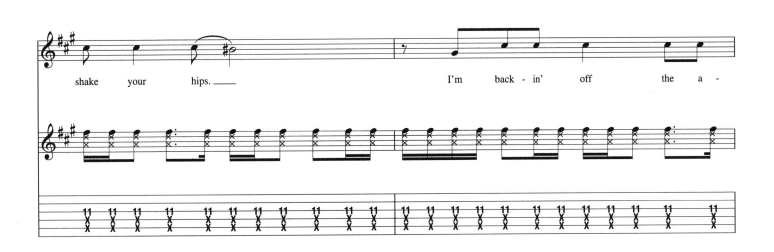

shake your hips. _ I'm back - in' off the a -

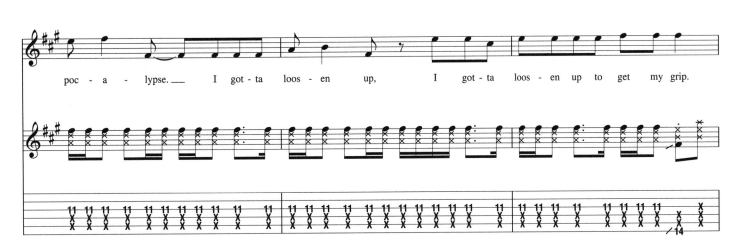

poc - a - lypse. _ I got - ta loos - en up, I got - ta loos - en up to get my grip.

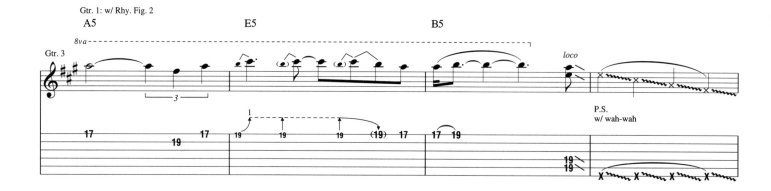

Free time

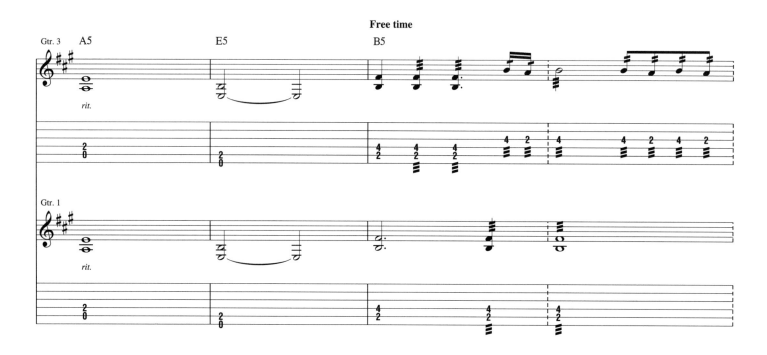

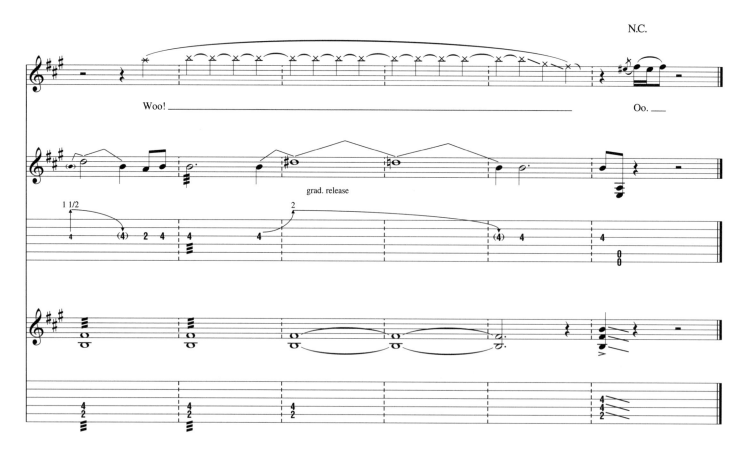

Storm in a Teacup

Words and Music by Anthony Kiedis, Flea, John Frusciante and Chad Smith

Gtr. 1: w/ Riff A (2 times)

try to be a la - dy, but you're walk - in' like a so - ur kraut.   Roo tay, woo tay, git __ ti, ga ta, goo tay.

Look a, look a, like a, like a, like you wan - na get some.   If you
Roo tay, woo tay, git __ ti, ga ta, goo tay.

nev - er tell a lie, then you nev - er have to play dumb.
Roo tay, woo tay, git __ ti, ga ta, goo tay.)

Gtr. 1

𝄋 Pre-Chorus

*Gm

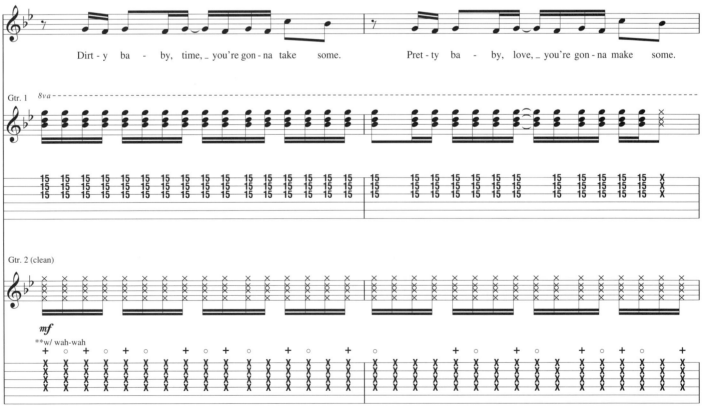

Dirt - y ba - by, time, _ you're gon - na take some.   Pret - ty ba - by, love, _ you're gon - na make some.

Gtr. 1 8va -

Gtr. 2 (clean)

mf
**w/ wah-wah

*Chord symbols reflect overall harmony.

** + = closed (toe down); ○ = open (toe up)

242

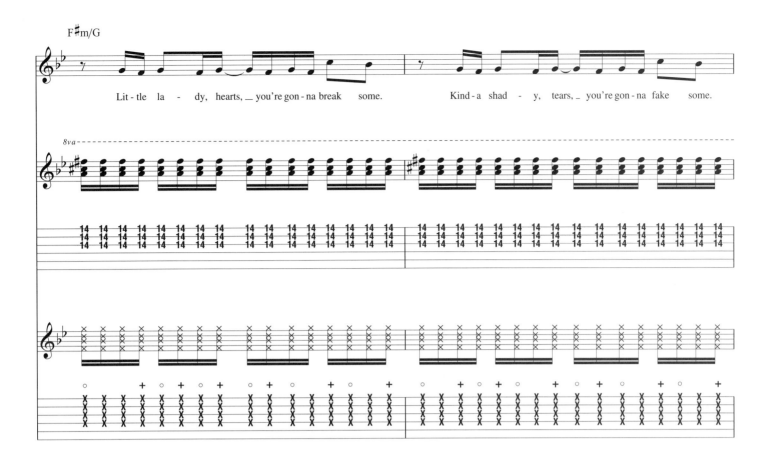

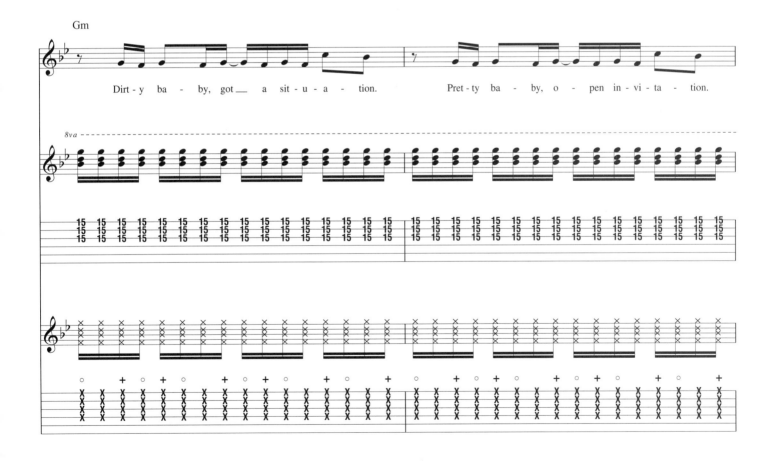

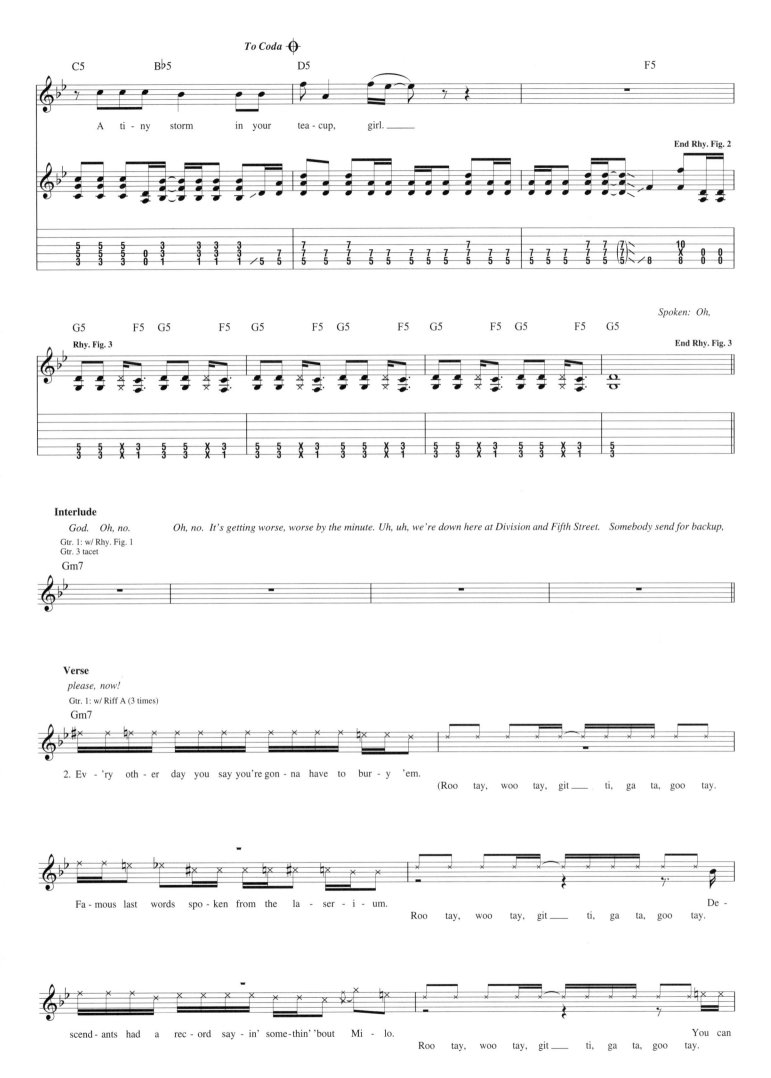

Gtr. 3: w/ Rhy. Fig. 3

Yeah.   Woo!   Yeah.   Woo!   Yeah.   Woo!   Yeah.

Interlude

Gtr. 1: w/ Riff A
Gtr. 4 tacet

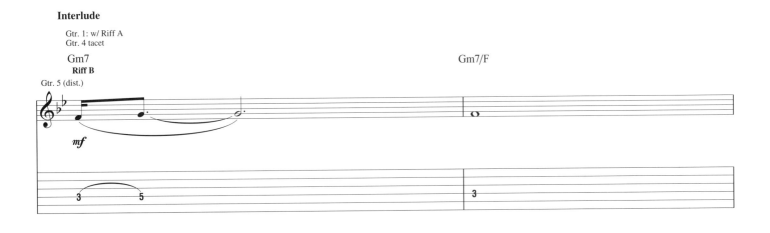

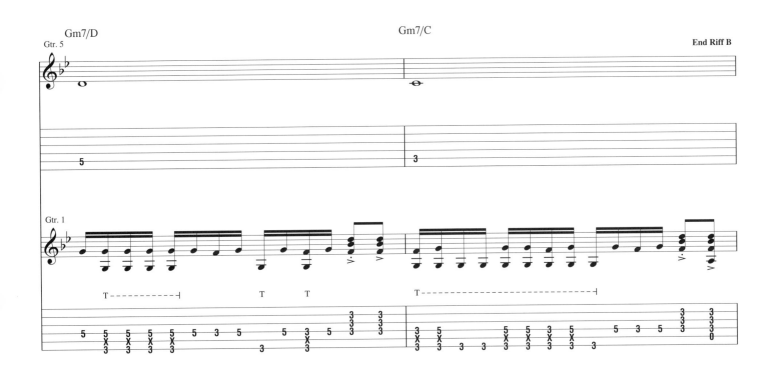

End Riff B

✛ Coda

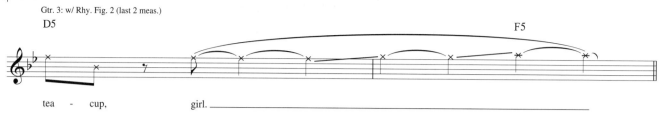

Outro-Guitar Solo

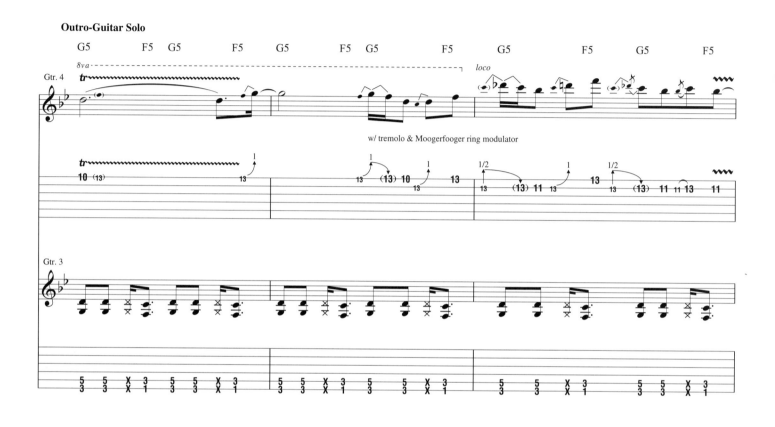

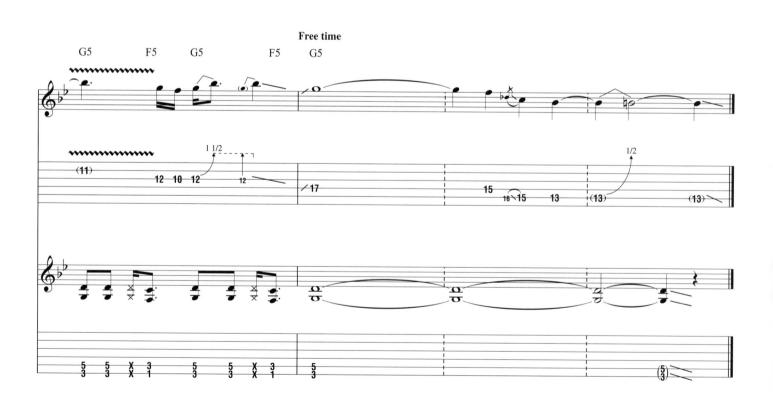

We Believe

Words and Music by Anthony Kiedis, Flea, John Frusciante and Chad Smith

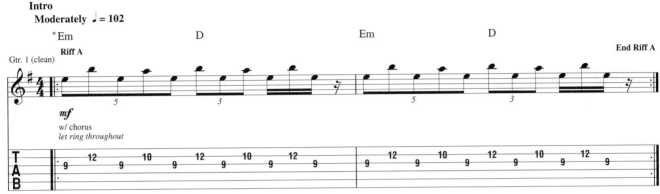

*Chord symbols reflect overall harmony.

Verse

1. The cur-tain is o-pen, a head to put dope in.

Now we will come clean it. The fu-ture, we've seen it.

No, no. I know, I said no, no. It's

like a dream that falls a-way in-to the night where we can play. On a train one hap-py day, two

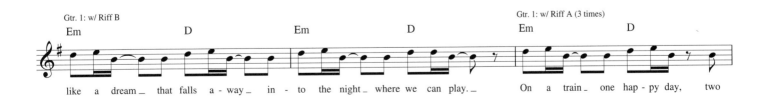

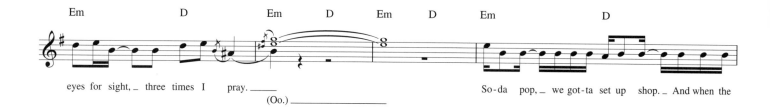

eyes for sight, _ three times I pray. _____
(Oo.) _____
So-da pop, _ we got-ta set up shop. _ And when the

Gtr. 1: w/ Riff B (2 times)

weath-er come, _ we got a pres-sure drop. _
We don't know, _ but ev-'ry day I go ____ to see what

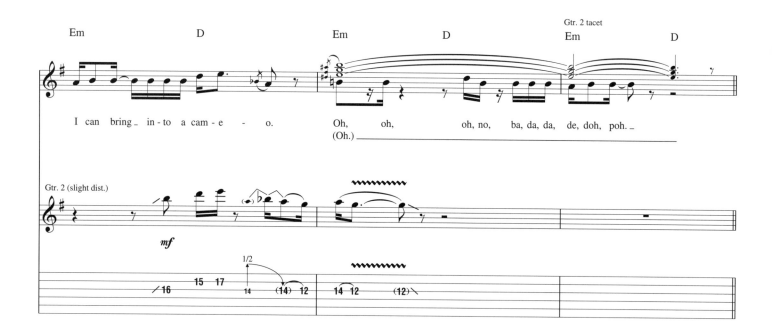

Gtr. 2 tacet

I can bring _ in-to a cam-e - o.
Oh, oh, oh, no, ba, da, da, de, doh, poh. _
(Oh.) _____

Gtr. 2 (slight dist.)

mf

Chorus

We be - lieve, _ we be - lieve. _

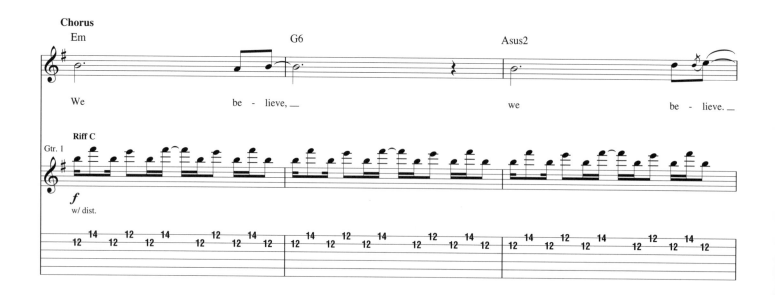

Riff C

Gtr. 1

f

w/ dist.

We be - lieve,_____
(Climb a tree for mon - key busi - ness, write a check out to for - give - ness.

*Refers to downstemmed voc. only.

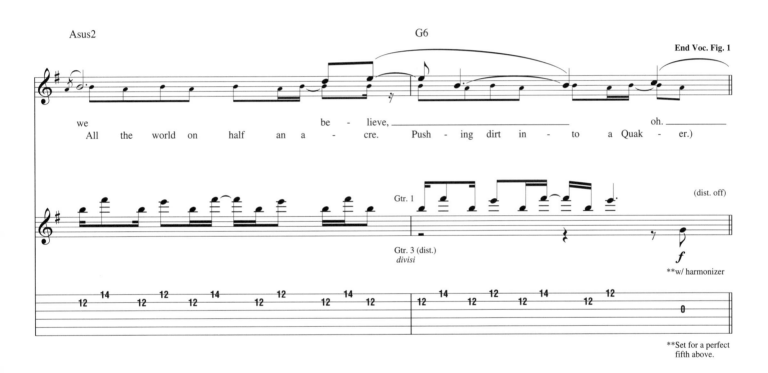

we be - lieve,_____ oh._____
All the world on half an a - cre. Push - ing dirt in - to a Quak - er.)

**Set for a perfect
fifth above.

Interlude

Gtr. 1: w/ Riff A (2 times)

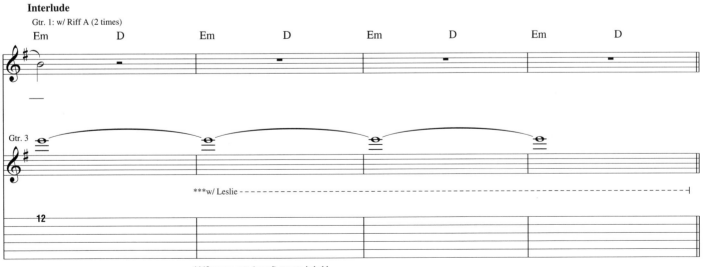

***Increase rate (speed) as note is held.

Verse

Gtr. 1: w/ Riff A (2 times)   Gtr. 3 tacet

2. The mis - sion, the meth - od, the down - fall ar - rest - ed. 'Cuz it's ___ not the first ___ time,

P.S.   (harmonizer & Leslie off)

Gtr. 1: w/ Riff B (2 times)

nor is ___ it the worst ___ time. No, no. ___ Oh, no, ___ ba, da, da,

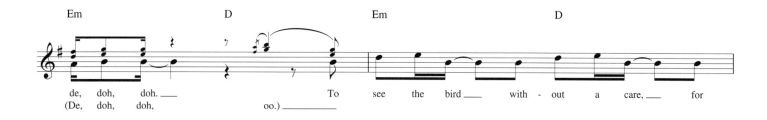

de, doh, doh. ___ To see the bird ___ with - out a care, ___ for
(De, doh, doh, oo.) ___

Gtr. 1: w/ Riff A (2 times)

in a word ___ it's nice out there. In a tree, ___ my ma - ma bear ___ will

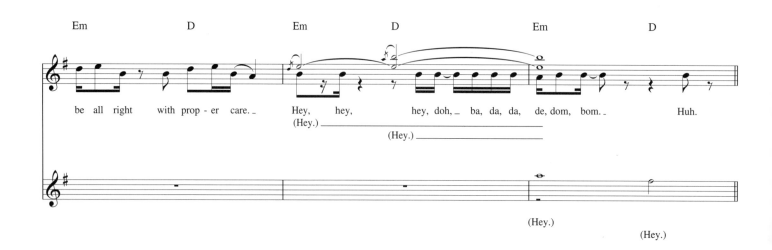

be all right with prop - er care. ___ Hey, hey, hey, doh, ___ ba, da, da, de, dom, bom. ___ Huh.
(Hey.) ___
(Hey.) ___

(Hey.)
(Hey.)

254

Turn It Again

Words and Music by Anthony Kiedis, Flea, John Frusciante and Chad Smith

Uh, you can dance for the sake of a gold - en day, take a chance on get-ting rid of what-ev-er's in ___ your way.

Next stop, big hop is turn - ing night in - to day.

Some-times when I'm ly - in' there all ___ a - lone, ___ I think of ev -'ry lit - tle noth-ing that we ___ could own

(Oo.) ___

*Refers to upstemmed voc. only.

to o - ver - throw all of you who have o - ver - grown. ___

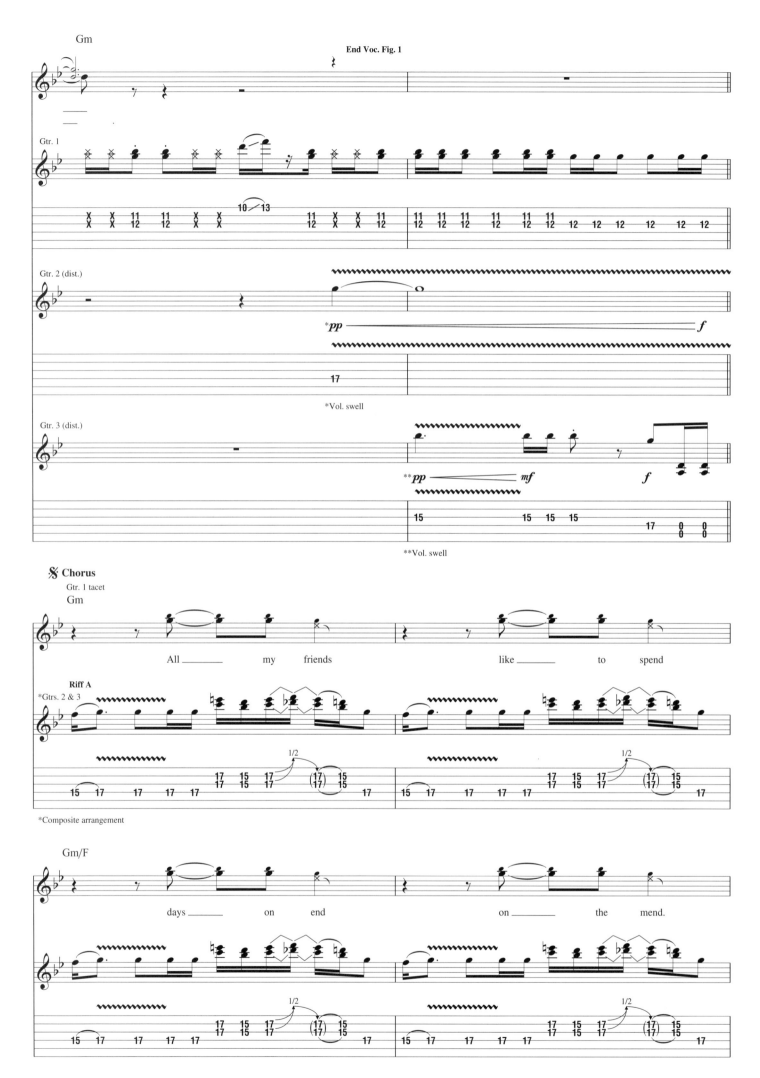

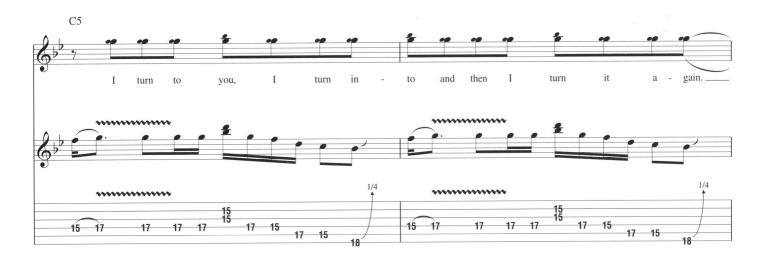

I turn to you, I turn in-to and then I turn it a - gain.

To Coda ⊕

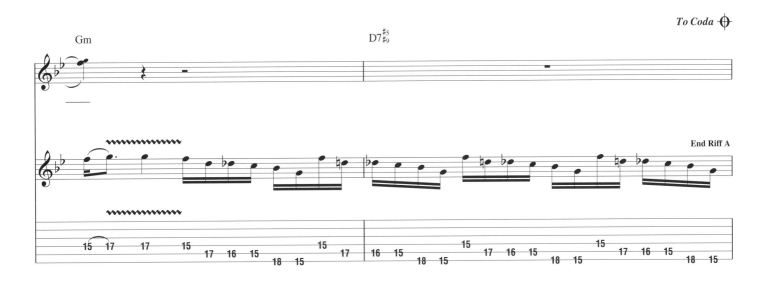

End Riff A

Gtrs. 2 & 3: w/ Riff A (1st 4 meas.)

Here — we go, all — we know, heav - y load, start — to float.

With - out a doubt, we turn it out and then we turn it a - gain. —

Riff B
Gtrs. 2 & 3

hold bend hold bend

End Riff B

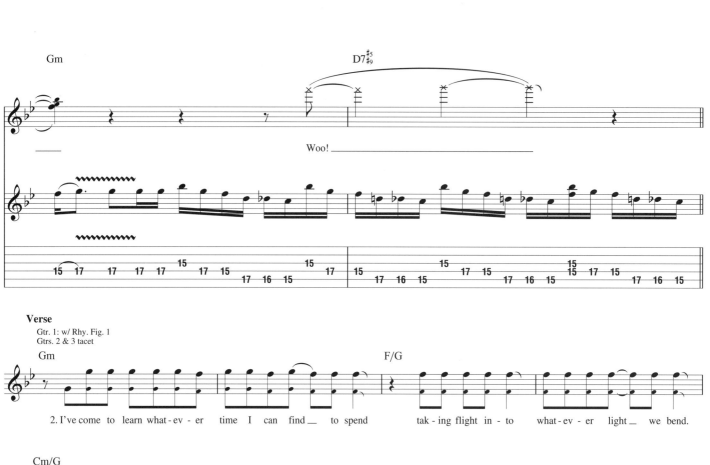

Verse
Gtr. 1: w/ Rhy. Fig. 1
Gtrs. 2 & 3 tacet

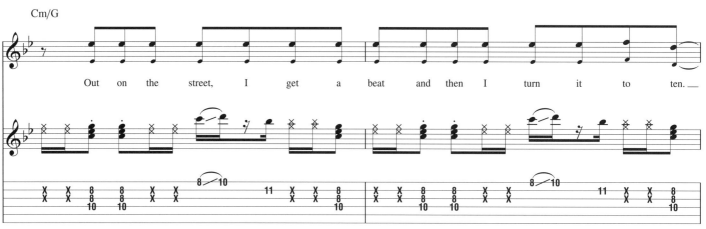

2. I've come to learn what-ev-er time I can find __ to spend tak-ing flight in-to what-ev-er light __ we bend.

Out on the street, I get a beat and then I turn it to ten. __

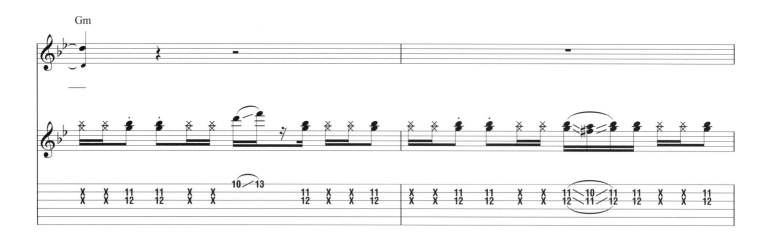

Bkgd. Voc.: w/ Voc. Fig. 1
Gtr. 1: w/ Rhy. Fig. 1

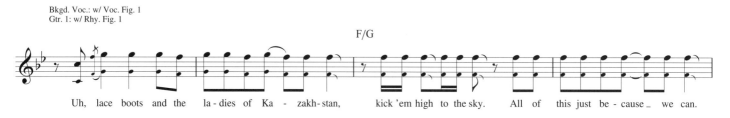

Uh, lace boots and the la-dies of Ka - zakh-stan, kick 'em high to the sky. All of this just be-cause __ we can.

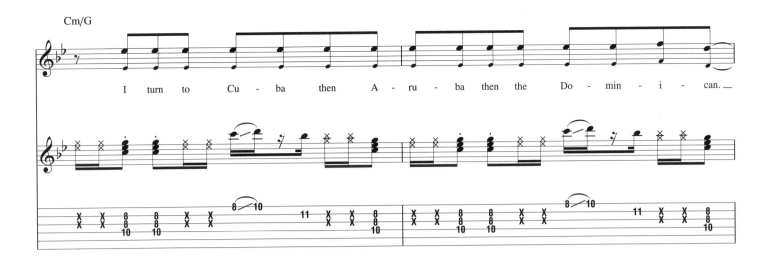

I turn to Cu - ba then A - ru - ba then the Do - min - i - can. _

D.S. al Coda

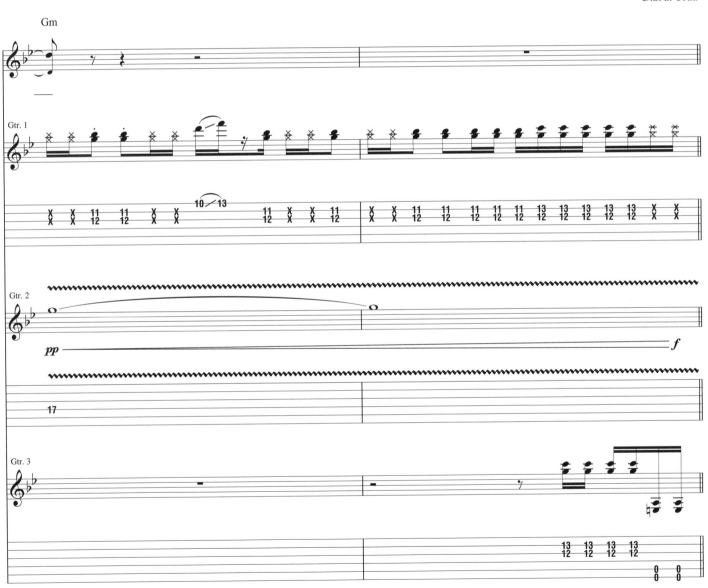

Coda

Here we go, all we know, heav-y load,

(Two things I want to say now. You made it all

start to float. With-out a doubt I turn it out and then we turn it a-gain.

o-kay now. I need to know that you are there.)

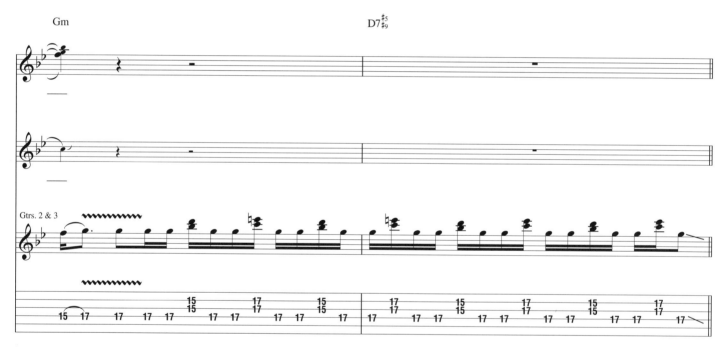

Bridge

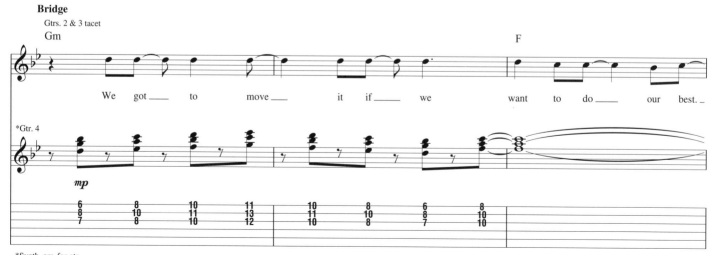

We got to move it if we want to do our best.

*Synth. arr. for gtr.

Verse

Gtr. 1: w/ Rhy. Fig. 1
Gtr. 4 tacet

3. I'm turn-in' down all the heav-y psy-chol - o-gy to cut a rug, and I

Gtr. 1: w/ Rhy. Fig. 2

make no a-pol - o-gy. I turn a cheek, I turn a key and then I turn it for free.

Gtr. 1: w/ Rhy. Fig. 1
Gtr. 5: w/ Rhy. Fig. 3

We've got-ta move it just a lit-tle to hit ___ the spot. A whirl-ing derv-ish in a

(Oo, ___

Gtr. 1: w/ Rhy. Fig. 2 (1st 2 meas.)

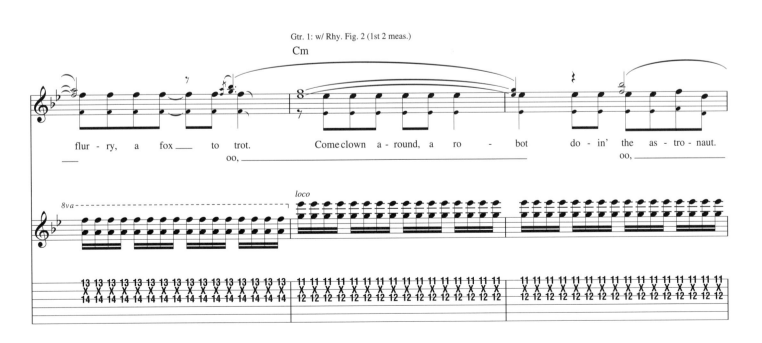

flur-ry, a fox ___ to trot. Come clown a-round, a ro-bot do-in' the as-tro-naut.

oo, ___ oo, ___

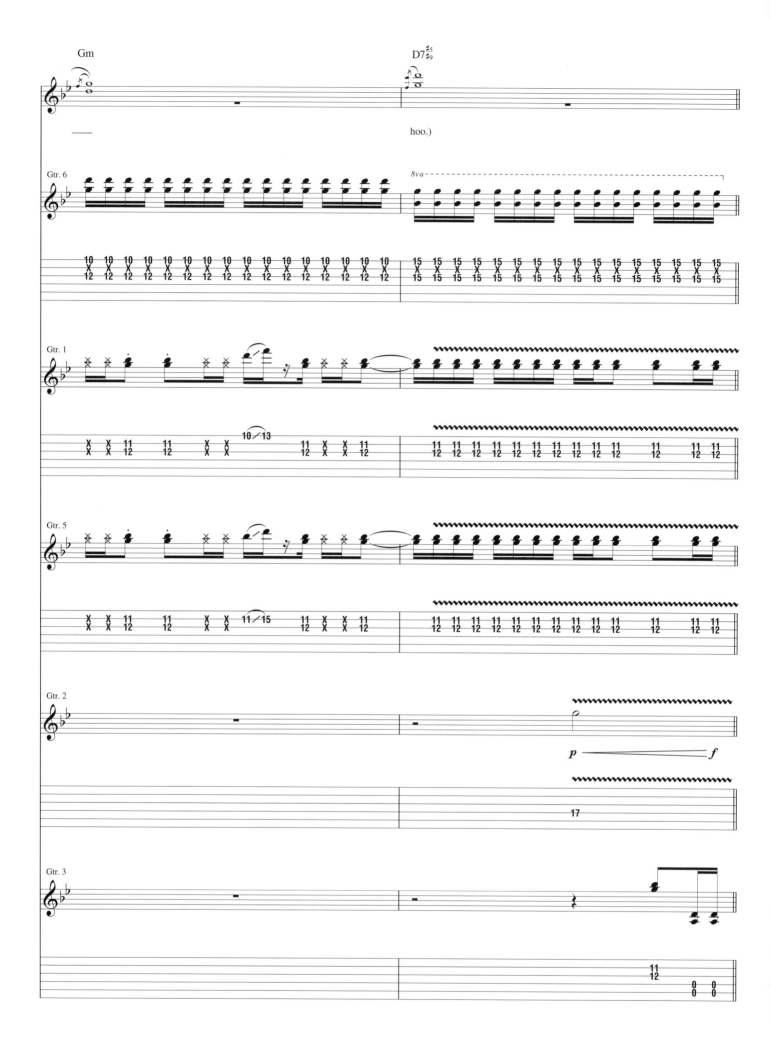

Chorus

Gtrs. 1, 5 & 6: tacet
Gtrs. 2 & 3: w/ Riff A (1 1/2 times)

All — my friends like — to spend days — on end on — the mend.

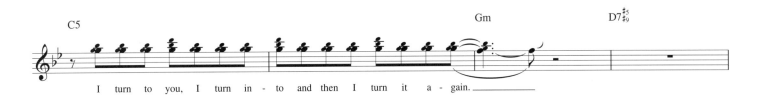

I turn to you, I turn in - to and then I turn it a - gain. _____

Here — we go, all — we know, heav - y load,

(Two things I want to say — now. You made it all —

Gtrs. 2 & 3: w/ Riff B

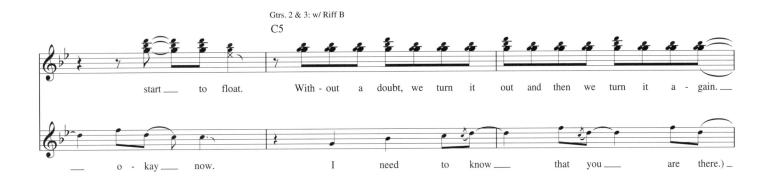

start — to float. With - out a doubt, we turn it out and then we turn it a - gain. —

— o - kay — now. I need to know — that you — are there.) _

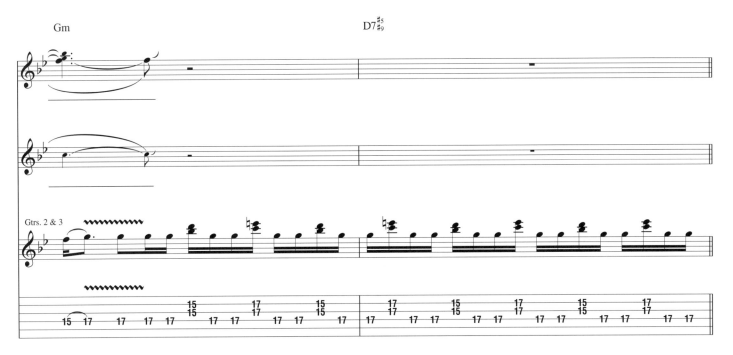

Gtrs. 2 & 3

Outro-Guitar Solo

Gtr. 3: w/ Riff A (1 1/2 times)

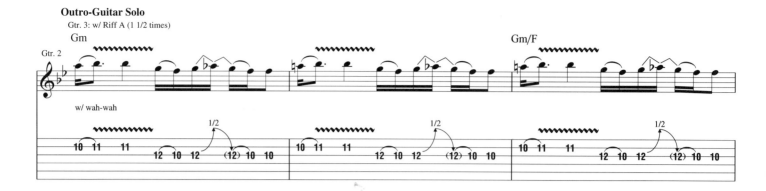

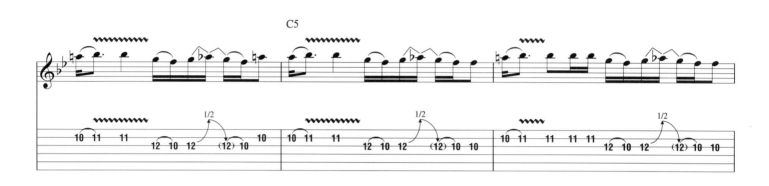

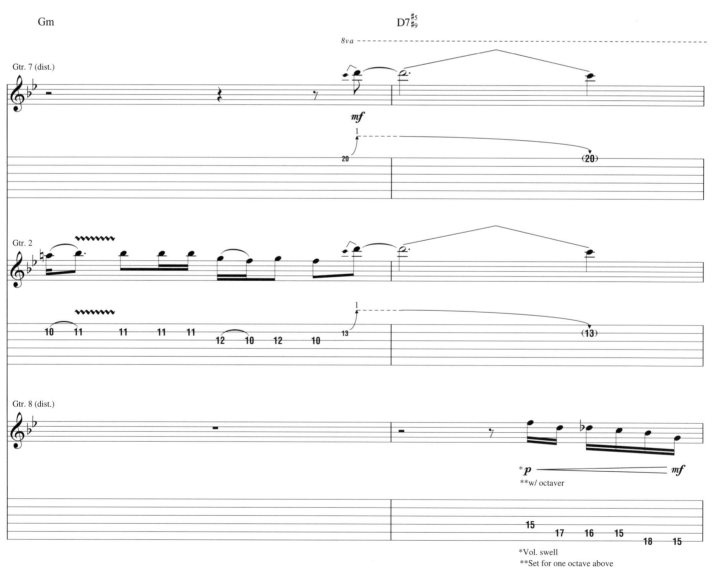

*Vol. swell
**Set for one octave above

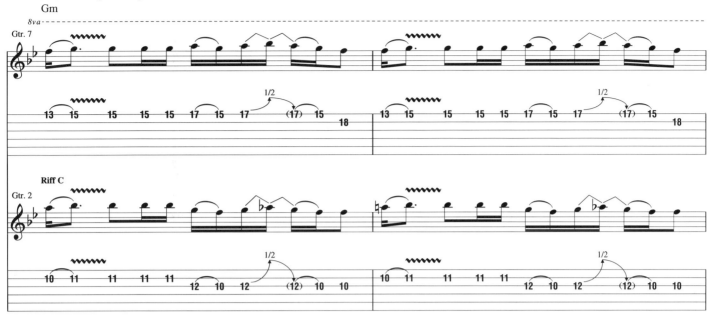

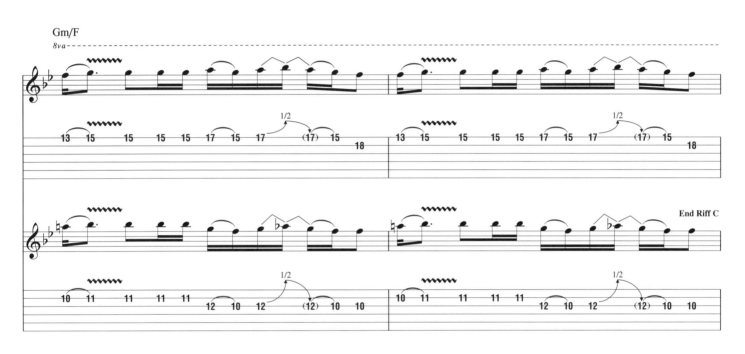

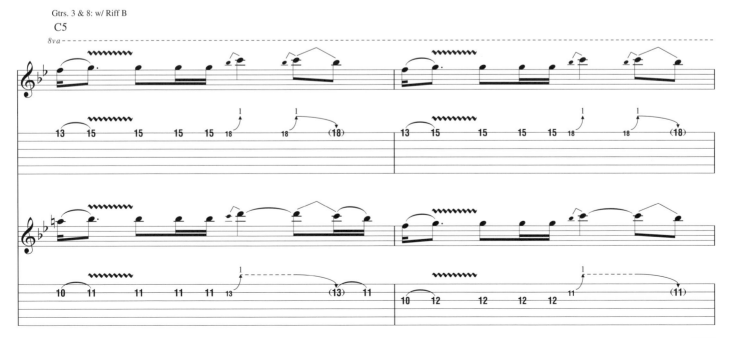

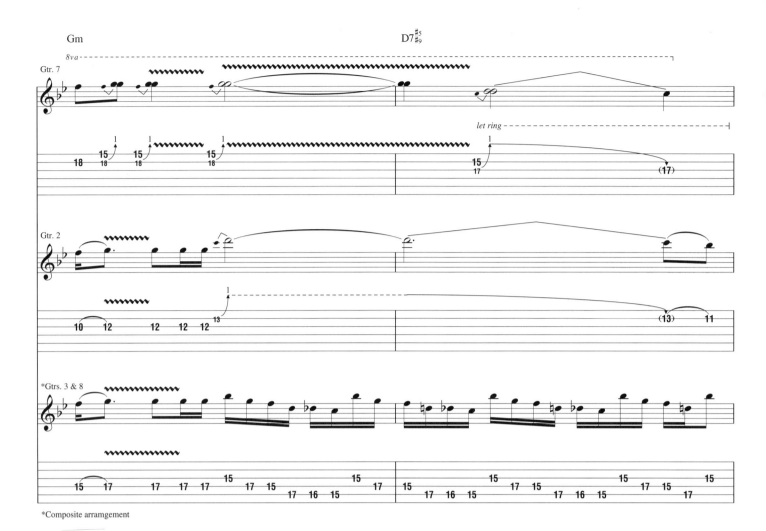

*Composite arramgement

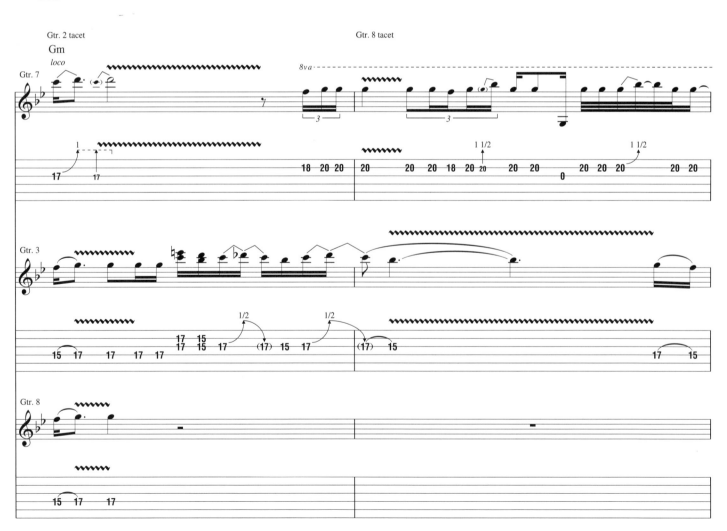

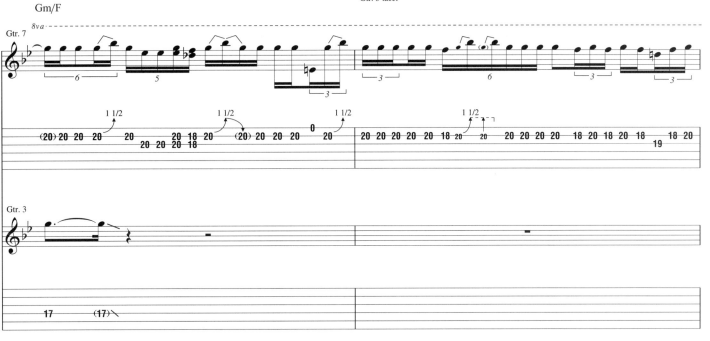

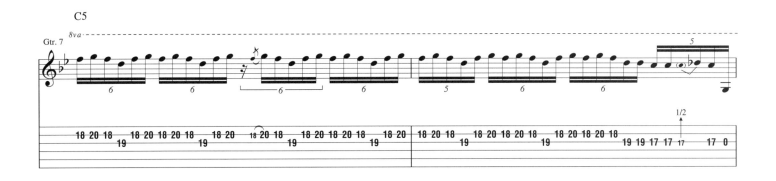

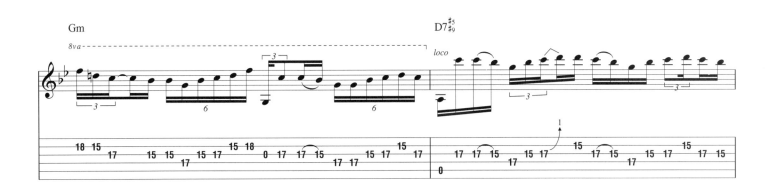

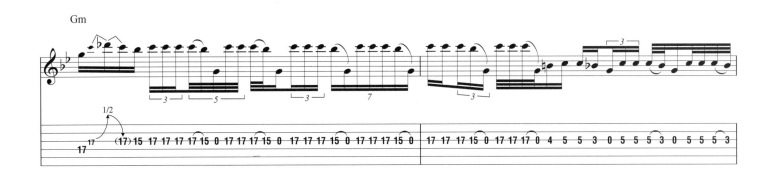

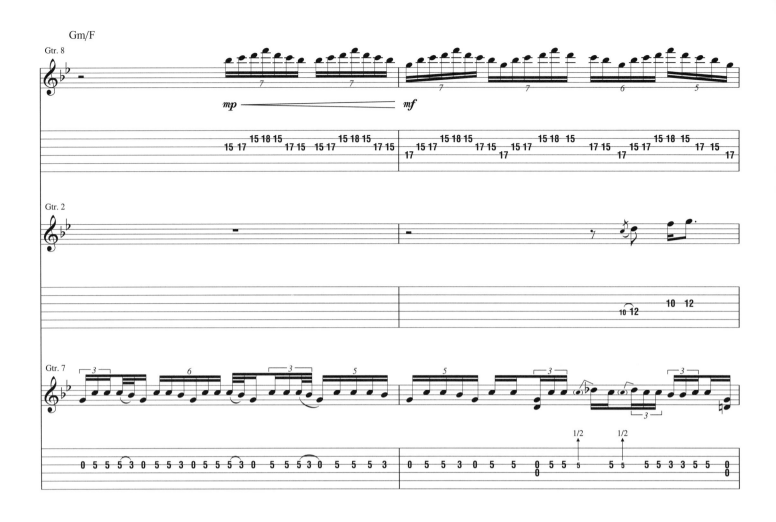

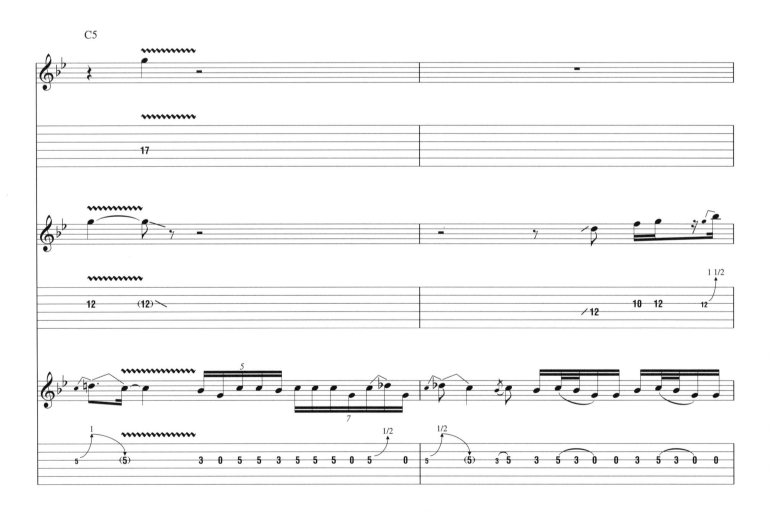

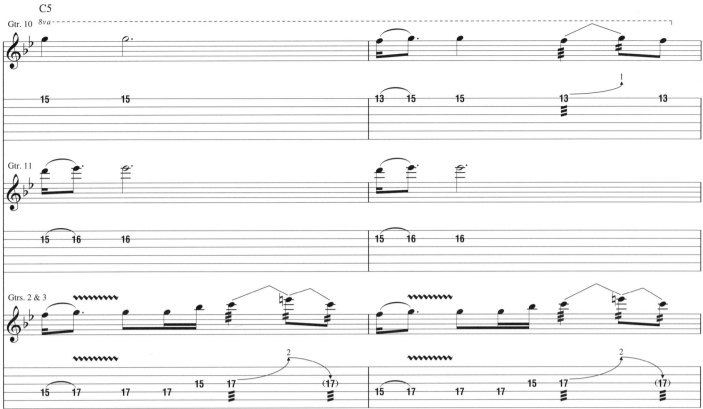

Death of a Martian

Words and Music by Anthony Kiedis, Flea, John Frusciante and Chad Smith

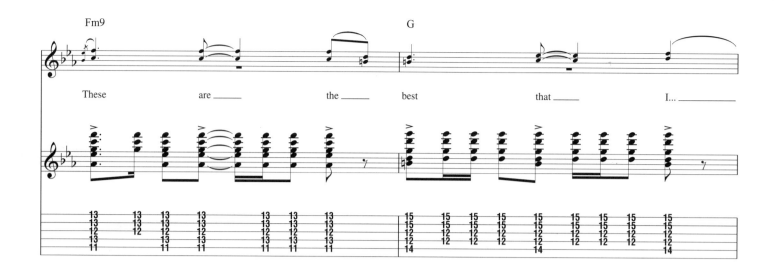

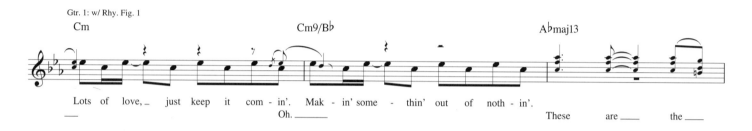

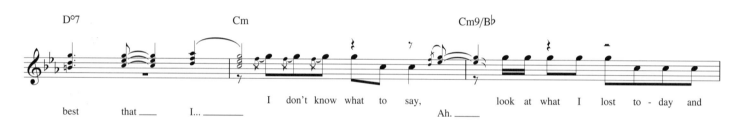

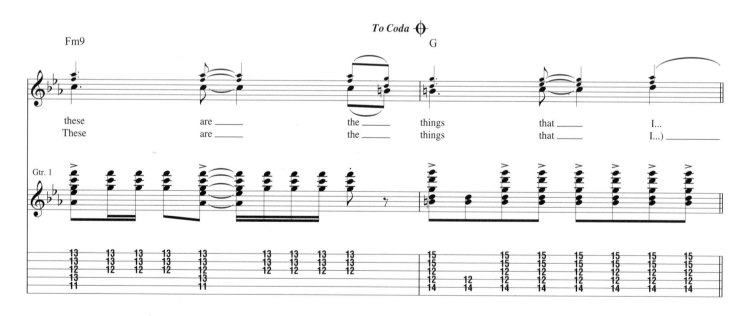

283

Outro

Gtrs. 1 & 2: w/ Riff C (8 times)

Spoken: She's got a sword in case though this is not her lord in case the one who can't afford to face her image is restord to grace. Disappeared.

No trace. Musky tears. Suitcase.   The down turn brave little burncub bearcareless turnip snare rampages pitch color pages....   down and

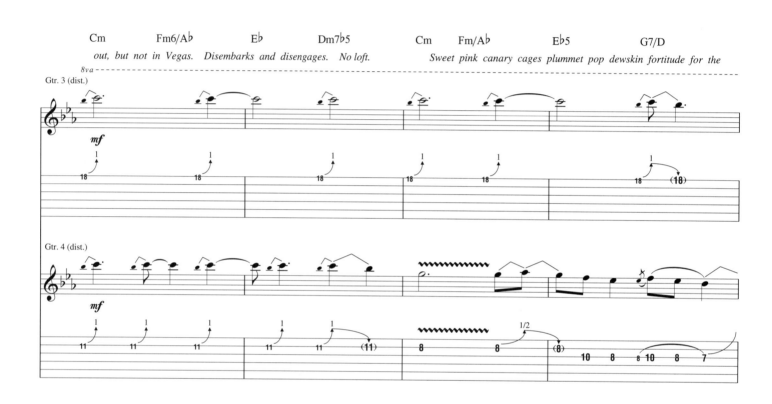

out, but not in Vegas. Disembarks and disengages. No loft.   Sweet pink canary cages plummet pop dewskin fortitude for the

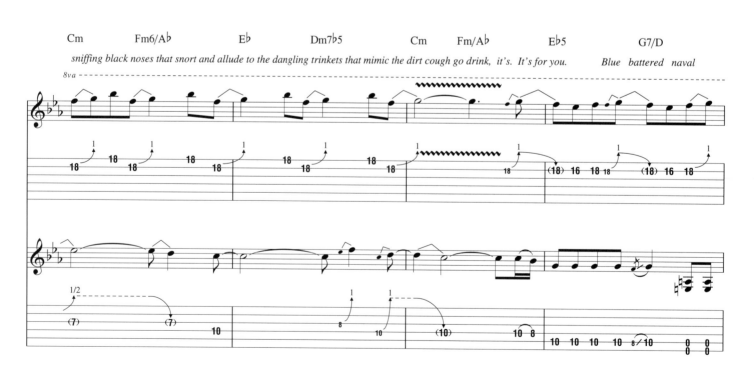

sniffing black noses that snort and allude to the dangling trinkets that mimic the dirt cough go drink, it's. It's for you.   Blue battered naval

stile touch bunny whose bouquet set a course for bloom without decay.   Get your broom and sweep echos of yesternight's fallen freckles...

Free time

a - way...

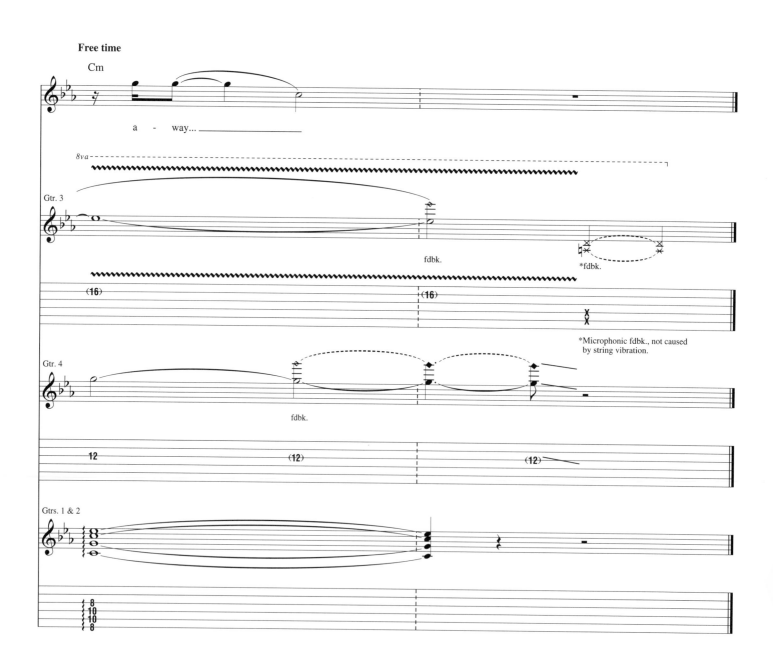

*Microphonic fdbk., not caused by string vibration.

Guitar Notation Legend

Guitar Music can be notated three different ways: on a *musical staff*, in *tablature*, and in *rhythm slashes*.

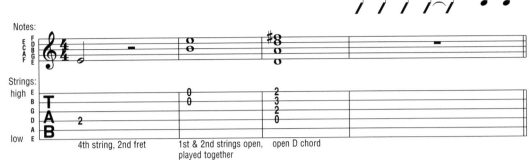

RHYTHM SLASHES are written above the staff. Strum chords in the rhythm indicated. Use the chord diagrams found at the top of the first page of the transcription for the appropriate chord voicings. Round noteheads indicate single notes.

THE MUSICAL STAFF shows pitches and rhythms and is divided by bar lines into measures. Pitches are named after the first seven letters of the alphabet.

TABLATURE graphically represents the guitar fingerboard. Each horizontal line represents a string, and each number represents a fret.

HALF-STEP BEND: Strike the note and bend up 1/2 step.

BEND AND RELEASE: Strike the note and bend up as indicated, then release back to the original note. Only the first note is struck.

HAMMER-ON: Strike the first (lower) note with one finger, then sound the higher note (on the same string) with another finger by fretting it without picking.

TRILL: Very rapidly alternate between the notes indicated by continuously hammering on and pulling off.

PICK SCRAPE: The edge of the pick is rubbed down (or up) the string, producing a scratchy sound.

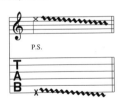

TREMOLO PICKING: The note is picked as rapidly and continuously as possible.

WHOLE-STEP BEND: Strike the note and bend up one step.

PRE-BEND: Bend the note as indicated, then strike it.

PULL-OFF: Place both fingers on the notes to be sounded. Strike the first note and without picking, pull the finger off to sound the second (lower) note.

TAPPING: Hammer ("tap") the fret indicated with the pick-hand index or middle finger and pull off to the note fretted by the fret hand.

MUFFLED STRINGS: A percussive sound is produced by laying the fret hand across the string(s) without depressing, and striking them with the pick hand.

VIBRATO BAR DIVE AND RETURN: The pitch of the note or chord is dropped a specified number of steps (in rhythm) then returned to the original pitch.

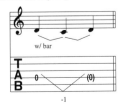

GRACE NOTE BEND: Strike the note and immediately bend up as indicated.

VIBRATO: The string is vibrated by rapidly bending and releasing the note with the fretting hand.

LEGATO SLIDE: Strike the first note and then slide the same fret-hand finger up or down to the second note. The second note is not struck.

NATURAL HARMONIC: Strike the note while the fret-hand lightly touches the string directly over the fret indicated.

PALM MUTING: The note is partially muted by the pick hand lightly touching the string(s) just before the bridge.

VIBRATO BAR SCOOP: Depress the bar just before striking the note, then quickly release the bar.

SLIGHT (MICROTONE) BEND: Strike the note and bend up 1/4 step.

WIDE VIBRATO: The pitch is varied to a greater degree by vibrating with the fretting hand.

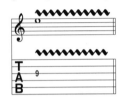

SHIFT SLIDE: Same as legato slide, except the second note is struck.

PINCH HARMONIC: The note is fretted normally and a harmonic is produced by adding the edge of the thumb or the tip of the index finger of the pick hand to the normal pick attack.

RAKE: Drag the pick across the strings indicated with a single motion.

VIBRATO BAR DIP: Strike the note and then immediately drop a specified number of steps, then release back to the original pitch.

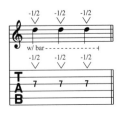

287

RECORDED VERSIONS®
The Best Note-For-Note Transcriptions Available

ALL BOOKS INCLUDE TABLATURE

00692015	Aerosmith – Greatest Hits $22.95
00690603	Aerosmith – O Yeah! (Ultimate Hits) $24.95
00690178	Alice in Chains – Acoustic $19.95
00694865	Alice in Chains – Dirt $19.95
00690387	Alice in Chains – Nothing Safe: The Best of the Box $19.95
00690812	All American Rejects – Move Along $19.95
00694932	Allman Brothers Band – Volume 1 ....$24.95
00694933	Allman Brothers Band – Volume 2 .....$24.95
00694934	Allman Brothers Band – Volume 3 .....$24.95
00690755	Alter Bridge – One Day Remains $19.95
00690609	Audioslave $19.95
00690804	Audioslave – Out of Exile $19.95
00690366	Bad Company – Original Anthology, Book 1 ...$19.95
00690503	Beach Boys – Very Best of $19.95
00690489	Beatles – 1 ....$24.95
00694929	Beatles – 1962-1966 ....$24.95
00694930	Beatles – 1967-1970 ....$24.95
00694832	Beatles – For Acoustic Guitar $22.95
00690110	Beatles – White Album (Book 1) $19.95
00690792	Beck – Guero $19.95
00692385	Berry, Chuck – $19.95
00692200	Black Sabbath – We Sold Our Soul for Rock 'N' Roll $19.95
00690674	Blink-182 ....$19.95
00690389	Blink-182 – Enema of the State $19.95
00690523	Blink-182 – Take Off Your Pants & Jacket ..$19.95
00690401	Bowie, David – Best of $19.95
00690764	Breaking Benjamin – We Are Not Alone ..$19.95
00690451	Buckley, Jeff – Collection $24.95
00690590	Clapton, Eric – Anthology $29.95
00690415	Clapton Chronicles – Best of Eric Clapton ..$18.95
00690074	Clapton, Eric – The Cream of Clapton ...$24.95
00690716	Clapton, Eric – Me and Mr. Johnson ...$19.95
00694869	Clapton, Eric – Unplugged $22.95
00690162	Clash – Best of The $19.95
00690593	Coldplay – A Rush of Blood to the Head ..$19.95
00690806	Coldplay – X & Y $19.95
00694940	Counting Crows – August & Everything After ..$19.95
00690401	Creed – Human Clay $19.95
00690352	Creed – My Own Prison $19.95
00690551	Creed – Weathered $19.95
00690648	Croce, Jim – Very Best of $19.95
00690572	Cropper, Steve – Soul Man $19.95
00690613	Crosby, Stills & Nash – Best of $19.95
00690777	Crossfade $19.95
00690289	Deep Purple – Best of $17.95
00690347	Doors, The – Anthology $22.95
00690348	Doors, The – Essential Guitar Collection ..$16.95
00690810	Fall Out Boy – From Under the Cork Tree ..$19.95
00690664	Fleetwood Mac – Best of $19.95
00690808	Foo Fighters – In Your Honor $19.95
00694920	Free – Best of $19.95
00690773	Good Charlotte – The Chronicles of Life and Death $19.95
00690601	Good Charlotte – The Young and the Hopeless $19.95
00690697	Hall, Jim – Best of $19.95
00694798	Harrison, George – Anthology $19.95
00690778	Hawk Nelson – Letters to the President ..$19.95
00692930	Hendrix, Jimi – Are You Experienced? ...$24.95
00692931	Hendrix, Jimi – Axis: Bold As Love $22.95
00690608	Hendrix, Jimi – Blue Wild Angel $24.95
00692932	Hendrix, Jimi – Electric Ladyland $24.95
00690017	Hendrix, Jimi – Live at Woodstock $24.95

00690602	Hendrix, Jimi – Smash Hits $19.95
00690692	Idol, Billy – Very Best of $19.95
00690688	Incubus – A Crow Left of the Murder ...$19.95
00690457	Incubus – Make Yourself $19.95
00690544	Incubus – Morningview $19.95
00690730	Jackson, Alan – Guitar Collection $19.95
00690721	Jet – Get Born $19.95
00690684	Jethro Tull – Aqualung $19.95
00690647	Jewel – Best of $19.95
00690751	John5 – Vertigo $19.95
00690271	Johnson, Robert – New Transcriptions ..$24.95
00699131	Joplin, Janis – Best of $19.95
00690427	Judas Priest – Best of $19.95
00690742	Killers, The – Hot Fuss $19.95
00694903	Kiss – Best of $24.95
00690780	Korn – Greatest Hits, Volume 1 ....$22.95
00690726	Lavigne, Avril – Under My Skin $19.95
00690679	Lennon, John – Guitar Collection $19.95
00690785	Limp Bizkit – Best of $19.95
00690781	Linkin Park – Hybrid Theory $22.95
00690782	Linkin Park – Meteora $22.95
00690783	Live, Best of $19.95
00690743	Los Lonely Boys $19.95
00690720	Lostprophets – Start Something $19.95
00694954	Lynyrd Skynyrd – New Best of $19.95
00690577	Malmsteen, Yngwie – Anthology $24.95
00690754	Manson, Marilyn – Lest We Forget $19.95
00694956	Marley, Bob – Legend $19.95
00694945	Marley, Bob – Songs of Freedom $24.95
00690748	Maroon5 – 1.22.03 Acoustic $19.95
00690657	Maroon5 – Songs About Jane $19.95
00120080	McLean, Don – Songbook $19.95
00694951	Megadeth – Rust in Peace $22.95
00690768	Megadeth – The System Has Failed $19.95
00690505	Mellencamp, John – Guitar Collection $19.95
00690646	Metheny, Pat – One Quiet Night $19.95
00690565	Metheny, Pat – Rejoicing $19.95
00690558	Metheny, Pat – Trio: 99>00 ....$19.95
00690561	Metheny, Pat – Trio > Live $22.95
00690040	Miller, Steve, Band – Young Hearts $19.95
00690769	Modest Mouse – Good News for People Who Love Bad News $19.95
00690786	Mudvayne – The End of All Things to Come ..$22.95
00690787	Mudvayne – L.D. 50 ....$22.95
00690794	Mudvayne – Lost and Found $19.95
00690611	Nirvana $22.95
00694883	Nirvana – Nevermind $19.95
00690026	Nirvana – Unplugged in New York $19.95
00690739	No Doubt – Rock Steady $22.95
00690807	Offspring, The – Greatest Hits $19.95
00694847	Osbourne, Ozzy – Best of $22.95
00690399	Osbourne, Ozzy – Ozzman Cometh $19.95
00694855	Pearl Jam – Ten $19.95
00690439	Perfect Circle, A – Mer De Noms $19.95
00690661	Perfect Circle, A – Thirteenth Step $19.95
00690499	Petty, Tom – Definitive Guitar Collection ..$19.95
00690731	Pillar – Where Do We Go from Here? ...$19.95
00690428	Pink Floyd – Dark Side of the Moon $19.95
00693864	Police, The – Best of $19.95
00694975	Queen – Greatest Hits $24.95
00690670	Queensryche – Very Best of $19.95
00694910	Rage Against the Machine $19.95
00690055	Red Hot Chili Peppers – Bloodsugarsexmagik $19.95
00690584	Red Hot Chili Peppers – By the Way ...$19.95

00690379	Red Hot Chili Peppers – Californication ..$19.95
00690673	Red Hot Chili Peppers – Greatest Hits $19.95
00690511	Reinhardt, Django – Definitive Collection ..$19.95
00690779	Relient K – MMHMM $19.95
00690643	Relient K – Two Lefts Don't Make a Right...But Three Do $19.95
00690631	Rolling Stones – Guitar Anthology $24.95
00690685	Roth, David Lee – Eat 'Em and Smile $19.95
00690694	Roth, David Lee – Guitar Anthology $24.95
00690749	Saliva – Survival of the Sickest $19.95
00690031	Santana's Greatest Hits $19.95
00690796	Schenker, Michael – Very Best of $19.95
00690566	Scorpions – Best of $19.95
00690604	Seger, Bob – Guitar Collection $19.95
00690530	Slipknot – Iowa $19.95
00690733	Slipknot – Vol. 3 (The Subliminal Verses) ..$19.95
00690691	Smashing Pumpkins Anthology $19.95
00120004	Steely Dan – Best of $24.95
00694921	Steppenwolf – Best of $22.95
00690655	Stern, Mike – Best of $19.95
00690689	Story of the Year – Page Avenue $19.95
00690520	Styx Guitar Collection $19.95
00120081	Sublime $19.95
00690519	SUM 41 – All Killer No Filler $19.95
00690771	SUM 41 – Chuck $19.95
00690767	Switchfoot – The Beautiful Letdown $19.95
00690815	Switchfoot – Nothing Is Sound $19.95
00690799	System of a Down – Mezmerize $19.95
00690531	System of a Down – Toxicity $19.95
00694824	Taylor, James – Best of $16.95
00690737	3 Doors Down – The Better Life $22.95
00690776	3 Doors Down – Seventeen Days $19.95
00690683	Trower, Robin – Bridge of Sighs $19.95
00690740	Twain, Shania – Guitar Collection $19.95
00699191	U2 – Best of: 1980-1990 ....$19.95
00690732	U2 – Best of: 1990-2000 ....$19.95
00690775	U2 – How to Dismantle an Atomic Bomb ..$22.95
00694411	U2 – The Joshua Tree $19.95
00660137	Vai, Steve – Passion & Warfare $24.95
00690370	Vaughan, Stevie Ray and Double Trouble – The Real Deal: Greatest Hits Volume 2 ..$22.95
00690116	Vaughan, Stevie Ray – Guitar Collection ...$24.95
00660058	Vaughan, Stevie Ray – Lightnin' Blues 1983-1987 ....$24.95
00694835	Vaughan, Stevie Ray – The Sky Is Crying ..$22.95
00690015	Vaughan, Stevie Ray – Texas Flood $19.95
00690772	Velvet Revolver – Contraband $22.95
00690071	Weezer (The Blue Album) $19.95
00690800	Weezer – Make Believe $19.95
00690447	Who, The – Best of $24.95
00690671	Williams, Dar – Best of $19.95
00690710	Yellowcard – Ocean Avenue $19.95
00690589	ZZ Top Guitar Anthology $22.95